FOOT CARE

The Essential Guide

Antonia
Mariconda

Footcare: The Essential Guide is also available in accessible formats for people with any degree of visual impairment. The large print edition and e-book (with accessibility features enabled) are available from Need2Know. Please let us know if there are any special features you require and we will do our best to accommodate your needs.

First published in Great Britain in 2012 by
Need2Know
Remus House
Coltsfoot Drive
Peterborough
PE2 9BF
Telephone 01733 898103
Fax 01733 313524
www.need2knowbooks.co.uk

Contents

Introduction

The Society of Chiropodists and Podiatrists reveals that up to 90% of British people will undergo some types of foot problems during the course of their lives. Most of these foot-related problems stem from the daily wear and tear we inflict upon our feet, however some are caused by congenital malformations and disabilities.

The human foot is one of the best-engineered parts of the body; a strong, mechanical structure with amazing capabilities.

Each foot has 33 joints, eight arches, 26 bones, more than a hundred muscles, ligaments and tendons that all work together to distribute body weight and allow movement. Unfortunately, many people pay no attention to their feet – until they start to hurt.

Foot disorders must be diagnosed and treated early, before they become very painful and incapacitating. In some cases, foot ailments can be the first sign of more serious medical problems. Your feet mirror your general health, so conditions like arthritis, diabetes, nerve and circulatory disorders can show their initial symptoms in your feet.

Whether you have heel pain or ingrown toenails, this essential guide can help you. Using medical research and expert advice from healthcare professionals, this book provides a concise and detailed guide to the diagnosis, treatment and management of some of the most common foot problems.

This book will:

- Explain in clear language the different types of foot problems that there are.

- Explain who can suffer from foot problems and why.

- Help you diagnose a foot problem if you think you may have one.

- Guide you through the various treatments available for foot problems, and how they work.

- Offer you expert advice from qualified healthcare professionals.

- Answer many of the frequently asked questions associated with foot problems.

- Offer you details of organisations, helplines and websites that give advice and information.

At the back of this book there is a help list detailing useful websites and organisations, a book list containing many helpful publications relating to foot problems and a glossary with medical terms clearly explained.

Most foot problems are easy to avoid and simple to treat, but it is important to visit a general practitioner (GP) or a chiropodist if you suffer from chronic or recurrent foot pain or dysfunction.

Foot Care: The Essential Guide guide will clearly inform you on all foot care problems. A foot problem treated early will save you from a lot of pain – and, in some cases, possibly even save your life.

Acknowledgements

Dr. Marco La Malfa

UKSH Group of Hospitals

Mr. Lehel Balint

Dr. David Eccleston

Andrew Stanley

Jacqueline Sutera

Sheldon Nadal

Hamish Dow

The Dow Clinic

Image Box PR

Scholl

Julian Caloianu

Disclaimer

This book is for general information about foot problems only. It is not intended to replace professional medical advice, although it can be used alongside it. Anyone with foot problems or who suspects they have a health concern should seek medical advice from a healthcare professional, such as their GP, in the first instance.

Part 1:

Understanding Our Feet

Chapter One

The Amazing Mechanical Structure of the Foot

The human foot is a strong and complex mechanical structure. The unsung heroes of the human body, your feet deserve to be worshipped and revered for the hard work they do. When you consider that a person walks over 75,000 miles (or nearly two and a half times round the world) in the average lifetime, it's easy to understand why a lot of people have foot problems.

The human foot is a combined structure of base and lever, supporting and balancing the body's weight while standing, as well as raising and moving the body forward when in motion.

A quarter of all the bones in the human body are located in the feet. There are 26 bones in our feet, each foot also has 33 joints, 19 muscles, 10 tendons and 107 ligaments. It is generally said by foot care professionals that when the bones of the feet are out of alignment, so is the rest of the body.

The foot can be subdivided into the hindfoot (the rear of the foot), the midfoot (the middle of the foot) and the forefoot (the front of the foot).

'The human foot is a combined structure of base and lever, supporting and balancing the body's weight while standing, as well as raising and moving the body forward when in motion.'

The breakdown of the foot structure

- Skeletal bones – The foot is composed of 26 skeletal bones held together by muscles, ligaments and tendons.

- Muscles – The foot has 32 muscles and tendons. Muscles of the foot and leg balance the body and control the levers. The muscles in the leg provide power for the foot and those in the foot itself are used mainly for balance and direction.

- Tendons – Tendons are strong inelastic 'ropes' which attach the muscles to the bones. They keep the dynamic balance and shape of the foot.

- Arch – An arch is a series of bones forming a rigid but curved structure, held together by ligaments. When pressure or weight is applied to the arch the ends tend to spread apart, but the ligaments, which do not give away under the pressure, hold it firmly in place. The foot has 1 main arch along the inside of the foot and 3 lesser arches: the metatarsal arch across the ball of the foot, the outer long arch down the outside of the foot and a short arch under the rear of the foot.

- Ligaments – The foot has 109 ligaments that serve as hinges to keep the bones and joints together. They are bands of 'ropes'. They are fibrous and strong but less elastic than muscles. Ligaments hold the bones together, particularly those of the arch, by keeping it in a firm, unyielding curve when weight is placed upon it. They maintain the static form of the foot.

- Weight distribution – Distribution of weight is concentrated upon six basic points of support provided by the bone framework. The heel bone takes about half the weight. Any abnormalities of the foot structure which upset the normal distribution of weight bearing will cause inconvenience and discomfort.

- Toes – The toes' function is to grip, clamping the feet to the walking surface. They give final propulsion as the foot completes a step, shifting weight to the other foot. Although the big toe carries part of the body weight with each step, no weight rests on the big toe as the body stands. The toes' gripping tendency helps to maintain balance and aid propulsion.

'The foot of a newborn child has only one bone. The rest of the foot is made up of cartilage.'

The growth of the human foot

The foot of a newborn child has only one bone. The rest of the foot is made up of cartilage. When a child reaches 3 years of age much of the cartilage has become bone and by age 6 all bones have taken shape but are still partly composed of cartilage.

The growth of the human foot comes in spurts. Studies show that during the first ten years of a child's life the foot grows about one-half inch a year. Between the ages of 10 and 20 the yearly growth rate slows down considerably, with maturity of growth arriving between the ages of 19 and 20.

Be warned, even at a late stage of development, incorrect posture, poor walking and incorrect shoes can still destroy the joint alignment of the foot structure and the bones themselves.

20 fascinating foot facts

While many of these foot facts are fun and interesting, some point out how important it is to take great care of your feet. Many maladies of your feet may point to more substantial health problems. If ignored, a few of these conditions can create debilitating and life-threatening conditions.

1. Three out of four people will experience foot health problems of varying degrees of severity at one time or another in their lives.

2. There are approximately 250,000 sweat glands in a pair of feet, and they excrete as much as half a pint of moisture each day.

3. The 52 bones in your feet make up about one quarter of all the bones in your body.

4. Women have about four times as many foot problems as men; lifelong patterns of wearing high heels are often the culprit.

5. The American Podiatric Medical Association says the average person takes 8,000 to 10,000 steps a day.

6. There are times when you're walking that the pressure on your feet exceeds your body weight; and when you're running, it can be three or four times your weight.

7. Your feet mirror your general health. Such conditions as arthritis, diabetes, nerve and circulatory disorders can show their initial symptoms in the feet. Foot ailments can be your first sign of more serious medical problems.

'There are approximately 250,000 sweat glands in a pair of feet, and they excrete as much as half a pint of moisture each day.'

8. Arthritis is the number one cause of disability in America. It limits everyday dressing, climbing stairs, getting in and out of bed or walking for about 7 million Americans.

9. About 60-70% of people with diabetes have mild to severe forms of diabetic nerve damage, which in severe forms can lead to lower limb amputations. Approximately 56,000 people a year lose their foot or leg to diabetes.

10. Only a small percentage of the population is born with foot problems. Many leading foot associations believe that eventual foot problems are caused by neglect, and a lack of awareness of proper care – including ill-fitting shoes.

11. Shoe size in Britain is measured in barleycorns, a unit of measurement that stretches back to Anglo-Saxon times. Based on the length of a grain of barley, there are three barleycorns to an inch, so each shoe size adds a third of an inch in length to a shoe.

12. The measuring device in shoe shops is called a Brannock Device, after the inventor who designed it in the twenties. Mr Brannock worked for the company all his life and ensured the devices were built to last. The firm is still going strong.

13. Most people do not wear the correct shoe size for their feet. According to David G Armstrong, Professor of Surgery at the William M Scholl College of Podiatric Medicine in Chicago, three-quarters of people wear the wrong size shoes. The reason for this may be that people stick to the size they were measured for when young and fail to realise that their feet change shape. People also like to get the most out of their footwear, and wear and re-wear them even if they no longer fit.

14. Going barefoot is best for your feet, joints and overall posture. A South African study in the podiatry journal *The Foot* in 2007, studied 180 modern humans from three different population groups (Sotho, Zulu and European) and compared them to 2,000-year-old skeletons. The researchers concluded that people had healthier feet and posture before the invention of shoes. The Zulu, who often go barefoot, had the healthiest feet of the modern humans.

'Most people do not wear the correct shoe size for their feet. The reason for this may be that people stick to the size they were measured for when young and fail to realise that their feet change shape.'

15. You can't tell anything about a man from the size of his feet. In 2002, nurses at St. Mary's Hospital and University College Hospital in London measured the foot size and penis length of 104 men and found there was no link between the two. Previous studies which had shown there was a mild correlation relied upon asking male subjects for their personal information rather than direct measurement.

16. Animals can be divided into 'plantigrades' – creatures that walk on the whole of their feet (like people, bears, baboons, alligators and frogs) – and 'digitigrade' – creatures that walk on their toes (like dogs, cats, birds and dinosaurs). A biped is something with two feet (from the Latin 'bi', (two), and 'ped' (foot)).

17. Butterflies taste with their feet, gannets incubate eggs under their webbed feet and elephants use their feet to hear – they pick up vibrations of the earth through their soles.

18. The word 'pedigree' is derived from the French phrase 'pied de gru', literally 'the foot of a crane', because the descent lines of family trees look like birds' feet.

19. Although centipedes have been extensively studied for more than a century, not one has ever been found that has exactly a hundred feet. Some have more, some less. The species which came closest to 100 was discovered in 1999. It had 96 legs, and is unique among centipedes in that it is the only known species with an even number of pairs of legs: forty-eight. All other centipedes have odd numbers of pairs of legs ranging between 15 and 191 pairs: that is, 30 and 382 legs.

20. 'Elvis foot' is climber's jargon for being so tired that your foot trembles on the rock (it is also known as 'disco knee').

Foot conditions

As a result of the hard work our feet carry out during our lifetime, a number of common foot conditions cause millions of people around the globe discomfort, pain and inconvenience. Here are some of the most commonly reported foot problems:

- Plantar fasciitis – Inflammation in the plantar fascia ligament along the bottom of the foot. Pain in the heel and arch, worse in the morning, are symptoms.

- Osteoarthritis of the feet – Age and wear and tear cause the cartilage in the feet to wear out. Pain, swelling and deformity in the feet are symptoms of osteoarthritis.

- Gout – An inflammatory condition in which crystals periodically deposit in joints, causing severe pain and swelling. The big toe is often affected by gout.

- Athlete's foot – A fungal infection of the feet, causing dry, flaking, red and irritated skin. Daily washing and keeping the feet dry can prevent athlete's foot.

- Rheumatoid arthritis – An autoimmune form of arthritis that causes inflammation and joint damage. Joints in the feet, ankle and toes may be affected by rheumatoid arthritis.

- Bunions (hallux valgus) – A bony prominence next to the base of the big toe that may cause the big toe to turn inward. Bunions may occur in anyone, but are often caused by heredity or ill-fitting footwear.

- Achilles tendon injury – Pain in the back of the heel may suggest a problem with the Achilles tendon. The injury can be sudden or a nagging daily pain (tendonitis).

- Diabetic foot infection – People with diabetes are vulnerable to infections of the feet, which can be more severe than they appear. People with diabetes should examine their feet daily for any injury or signs of developing infection such as redness, warmth, swelling and pain.

- Swollen feet (oedema) – A small amount of swelling in the feet can be normal after prolonged standing and is common in people with varicose veins. Foot oedema can also be a sign of heart, kidney or liver problems.

- Calluses – A build-up of tough skin over an area of frequent friction or pressure on the feet. Calluses usually develop on the balls of the feet or the heels and may be uncomfortable or painful.

- Corns – Like calluses, corns consist of excessive tough skin build-up at areas of excessive pressure on the feet. Corns typically have a cone shape with a point, and can be painful.

- Heel spurs – An abnormal growth of bone in the heel, which may cause severe pain during walking or standing. People with plantar fasciitis, flat feet or high arches are more likely to develop heel spurs.

- Ingrown toenails – One or both sides of a toenail may grow into the skin. Ingrown toenails may be painful or lead to infections.

- Fallen arches (flat feet) – The arches of the feet flatten during standing or walking, potentially causing other feet problems. Flat feet can be corrected with shoe inserts (orthotics), if necessary.

- Nail fungal infection (onychomycosis) – Fungus creates discolouration or a crumbling texture in the fingernails or toenails. Nail infections can be difficult to treat.

- Mallet toes – The joint in the middle of a toe may become unable to straighten, causing the toe to point down. Irritation and other feet problems may develop without special footwear to accommodate the mallet toe.

- Metatarsalgia – Pain and inflammation in the ball of the foot. Strenuous activity or ill-fitting shoes are the usual causes.

- Claw toes – Abnormal contraction of the toe joints, causing a claw-like appearance. Claw toe can be painful and usually requires a change in footwear.

- Fracture – The metatarsal bones are the most frequently broken bones in the feet, either from injury or repetitive use. Pain, swelling, redness and bruising may be signs of a fracture.

- Plantar wart – A viral infection in the sole of the foot that can form a callus with a central dark spot. Plantar warts can be painful and difficult to treat.

- Morton's neuroma – A growth consisting of nerve tissue often between the third and fourth toes. A neuroma may cause pain, numbness and burning, and often improves with a change in footwear.

Summing Up

- The foot bone anatomy is truly an amazing structure of the body.

- The foot can be divided into three categories: the hindfoot (rear), the midfoot (middle) and the forefoot (front).

- The structure and function of the foot is one of the most wonderful biological mechanisms of our body.

- A quarter of all the bones in our body are located in our feet.

- Up to 90% of British people will suffer from foot problems during the course of their lives

- The hard work our feet undertake throughout our lifetimes, leave us susceptible to foot problems such as: plantar fasciitis, bunions, foot oedema, nail fungal infections, plus many more.

Need2Know

Chapter Two

Common Foot Problems by Age

There are many foot problems that can occur in all age groups. The following list summarises the most common foot problems that are seen in each age group.

A detailed explanation of each foot problem listed in this chapter can be found in Part 2 of this guide, or please see our glossary.

Be sure to see your healthcare professional as soon as a problem occurs.

Newborns, infants and toddlers

Congenital malformations

A birth defect is a commonly used term for a 'congenital malformation'; this is a physical abnormality which is recognisable at birth.

Birth defects of the foot are the most common problems that are treated in infants and newborns.

Common types of birth defects include:

* Excessive flat or high arched feet.

* A clubfoot deformity.

* Too many toes, or webbed toes.

* A mal-positioned forefoot or heel.

'Birth defects of the foot are the most common problems that are treated in infants and newborns.'

▪ Disfigured toes and/or missing toes.

Today, most birth defects of the feet can be corrected. At birth, a newborn's feet should be examined by a doctor. Your child's doctor should also evaluate your child's feet on an annual basis to look for other foot problems throughout childhood.

Walking problems

Another common problem amongst this age group is walking problems; that would include children who are late walkers, children who trip and fall often, or children who do not place their feet in the correct position when walking, this is also known as 'toe walking'.

'Going barefoot is not only enjoyable, it's actually very healthy for the initial development of young feet.'

New parents are often very concerned about the health of their children early in life. Attention is usually focused on their inquisitive eyes, grasping hands and developing teeth. But what attention is paid to their still-developing feet? Often far too little, especially considering these are the appendages that will carry the weight of their body through a lifetime.

Only a small percentage of the world's population is actually born with foot problems. Rather, foot problems often arise later in life due to neglect and a lack of proper care and development earlier in life. During your child's first year, their feet will be incredibly soft and pliable. As such, any abnormal, repetitive pressures can easily cause the foot to deform. This is why foot specialists consider the first year to be the most important in the development of the feet.

The ideal conditions: children and footcare

Going barefoot is not only enjoyable, it's actually very healthy for the initial development of young feet. Studies show that walking barefoot early in life actually helps feet form properly and aids in musculature growth. By allowing the toes freedom to perform their natural 'grasping' actions, the feet naturally develop strength and coordination.

Of course, going barefoot is isn't always practical. When walking outside or on rough surfaces, babies' feet need to be covered. Their soft, tender skin needs protection from the dangers of infection through accidental cuts and abrasions. This is when proper footwear becomes very important.

Proper footwear: children

When choosing footwear to protect young, developing feet, experts agree you should look for the following qualities:

- Lightweight – Footwear should not be heavy or impede the child's movement in any way.

- Flexible/Soft – Footwear should not restrict important toe and foot mobility, nor should it bind the growing feet in any way.

- Breathable – Footwear should be constructed of breathable natural materials, such as leather, to promote healthy conditions around the feet.

- Flat – Footwear should not have any arch support. It should simulate barefoot conditions.

By following these simple guidelines, and measuring for a proper fit, your child's feet will be off to a healthy start.

Adolescent

The developing body of an adolescent can cause a young person to suffer a variety of foot problems. For a detailed explanation of each foot problem in the following list, please see Part 2.

Skin and nail problems that occur in adolescence are:

- Plantar warts (verrucas).

- Ingrown nails.

- Athlete's foot.

- Traumatic injuries (ankle sprains etc.).

- Growing pains.

Teen tips for a fabulous pedicure

Everyone needs a little foot pampering from time to time. Whether you're getting your toes ready for prom, prepping for beach season, or just want to splash on a bright colour before a hot date, grooming your feet should be done frequently to not only keep feet looking good, but also to ensure proper foot health.

Here are a few pointers to keep in mind next time you get a pedicure at home or at a salon:

- Don't shave your legs before receiving a pedicure. Resist the urge to have smooth legs, at least until afterward. Freshly shaven legs or small cuts on your legs may allow bacteria to enter your body.

- Do take your own pedicure utensils to the salon. Why? Because bacteria and fungus can move easily from one person to the next if the salon doesn't use proper sterilisation techniques.

- Don't allow salons to use a foot razor to remove dead skin. Using a razor can result in permanent damage if used incorrectly and can easily cause infection if too much skin is removed.

- Do use a pumice stone, foot file or exfoliating scrub when eliminating thick, dead skin build-up, also known as calluses, on the heel, ball and sides of the foot. Be sure to soak your feet in warm water for at least five minutes and then use the stone, scrub or foot file.

- Don't apply nail polish to cover up discoloured nails. Thick and discoloured toenails could be a sign of a fungal infection. Nail polish locks out moisture and doesn't allow the nail bed to 'breathe'. If you think you have a toenail infection, schedule an appointment with a podiatrist immediately to get it checked out.

- Do gently run a wooden or rubber manicure stick under your nails. This helps keep your nails clean and removes the dirt, glitter and other types of build-up you may not be able see

Adult

An adult can suffer a variety of foot ailments, here are some common problems:

- Acquired foot deformities – Due to the amount of the forces that are placed on the foot during walking and standing, the foot will undergo structural changes that can lead to muscle imbalances and joint misalignment. The most common acquired foot deformities are bunions, hammer toes and bone spurs.

- Overuse injuries – Overuse injuries involve putting a part of the foot through excessive tension or pulling which in turn results in an injury. The types of overuse injuries most commonly treated are plantar fasciitis, Achilles tendonitis, sesamoiditis, metatarsal stress fracture and Morton's neuroma.

- Shoe complications – Shoe complications involve placing too much pressure on the skin or positioning the foot in the wrong way while in the shoe, this can result in injury to the skin, tendons and/or bone. Wearing the wrong shoes can also cause corns and calluses, blisters and metatarsalgia (this is where the bone in the ball of the foot hurts with weight bearing).

- Natural wear and tear – Natural wear and tear complications are where the joints in the body becoming worn and painful.

- Systemic foot complications – Systemic foot complications are where the body is not functioning properly or there is a health issue that can result in a foot complication. Systemic diseases that can cause foot problems include diabetes, gout and skin allergies.

- Nail and skin infections – Nail fungal infections are very common in the adult population, these can include athlete's foot infections.

- Exercise-related problems – Because of the need for the muscle to be able to be flexible through the full range of motion, many injuries are caused from a lack of a warm-up before starting exercise or sports, or from an inappropriate technique or movement while performing sports. In the foot and ankle, exercise-related problems are very commonly treated. These include: plantar fasciitis, Achilles tendonitis and peroneal tendonitis.

'Wearing the wrong shoes can also cause corns and calluses, blisters and metatarsalgia.'

The ageing foot and older adults

The ability to walk comfortably without pain is a key part of ageing successfully. Foot problems are common among older adults and can lead to both pain and disability, and almost always cause difficulty walking for older adults. When foot problems limit your activity and do not get better, a visit to your doctor or podiatrist is in order.

One thing that doesn't shrink when people get older are the feet – they enlarge. More specifically, they flatten.

The feet's tendons and ligaments lose some of their elasticity and don't hold the bones and joints together as tidily. When combined with other ageing-related changes, the feet can encounter limits to how much use – or abuse – they can take.

'One thing that doesn't shrink when people get older are the feet – they enlarge. More specifically, they flatten.'

Dr. Steven Pribut, a podiatrist at George Washington University Medical Center in Washington DC, estimates that some people over the age of 40 can gain half a shoe size every 10 years.

The changes that take place in the foot are like those that take place in the rest of our body as we age. With time, tissues weaken and muscle mass declines and our bodies lose that youthful bounce and vigour.

Gravity gradually overwhelms the older, less resilient ligaments in the weight-bearing feet, but not in the free-floating hands. It also squeezes fluid from leaky veins in the lower extremities, contributing to swelling.

Looser tendons and ligaments mean more than the need for bigger shoes. As the front of the foot widens and the arch lowers, the foot becomes not only longer but more flexible and flatter, letting the ankle roll inward and increasing the chance of sprains.

Then there's the constant force of bearing weight that causes the fat pads cushioning the bottom of the feet to thin out.

'Even if you get fatter and heavier, the fat pads still get thinner,' says Dr. Mark Caselli, an adjunct professor at the New York College of Podiatric Medicine in New York City. When this happens, they can absorb less shock, which can make feet sore and painful after time.

The loss of padding can also cause corns and calluses on your balls and heels, Caselli says, 'Which for athletes can cause problems when performing activities. Patients report that they feel like they are walking directly on their foot bones.'

As the foot becomes wider, longer and less padded, the plantar fascia tendon that runs along the length of the sole and forms the arch becomes stretched, contributing to the lowering of the arch. A lower arch contributes to bunions, sometimes painful, bony prominences sticking out from the big toe.

Foot flattening has the added disadvantage of pulling the big toe up. This can cause pain in its own right, but if a big toe is sticking up and in a too-tight shoe, it can rub against the top of the shoe, thickening the toenail and possibly damaging it.

Osteoarthritis, rheumatoid arthritis and osteoporosis can pester joints and bones of the feet as well, especially in the big toe, already hampered by tendons and ligaments pulling it up. These conditions can cause damage to bones and joints, and thin bones are more prone to stress fractures.

The most obvious age-related change, however, overlooked by many people, is wearing the wrong size shoe. When too-tight shoes are combined with declining circulation – which means less sensitive feet – the skin of the feet can suffer undue friction. This friction causes hard bumps of skin – calluses and corns – that can also be painful.

There's plenty of help for ageing feet, though. The right size shoes – properly fitted, with good support and cushioning – are key. Even so, experts say older feet won't have the same stamina that they did in their youth.

Shoes should have good cushioning in the heel to make up for the loss of natural padding, and the widest part of the foot – usually the front – should fit the widest part of the shoe

Many experts recommend keeping the leg muscles in good shape. Out-of-shape calf muscles can torment the plantar fascia and Achilles tendons. Basic stretching and weight-bearing exercises help prevent muscle and bone loss and improve circulation.

'Many experts recommend keeping the leg muscles in good shape. Basic stretching and weight-bearing exercises help prevent muscle and bone loss and improve circulation.'

Summing Up

- Foot problems can affect people of all ages.
- In children they commonly appear as:
  - Flat feet.
  - Ingrown toenails.
  - Warts.
  - Toe gait.
  - Sports injuries.
- In adults the following problems are regular in occurrence:
  - Sports injuries.
  - Overuse.
  - Wearing the wrong types of shoes.
- In women the following seem to be a problem:
  - Wearing high heels.
  - Narrow shoes.
  - Being on the feet in thin-soled shoes.
- In the elderly, advanced conditions cause discomfort and issues, these include:
  - Bunions.
  - Hammer toes.
  - Callus formation.
- Most people, due to different activities, are susceptible at different ages to foot issues.
- No matter what age, or whatever the foot problem may be, it is best to seek medical expertise from a GP or a foot specialist to ensure your problem is getting the best treatments and solutions available to you.

Need2Know

Chapter Three

What Your Feet Say About Your Health

The Ancient Greek philosopher Socrates once claimed, 'When our feet hurt, we hurt all over'.

'Your feet are a mirror of your health,' says Dr. Sheldon Nadal, a Toronto-based podiatrist with 30 years' experience treating foot problems. 'If you have poor circulation, if you smoke, if you have a circulatory disease or poor nutrition, it's going to affect your feet.'

Find out what signs and symptoms you should be aware of, and how they might impact your health and wellbeing.

The symptoms: what do they mean?

- Dry or cracking skin – The face isn't the only place you'll see the signs of ageing. As we get older, skin becomes thinner and drier on the feet too. While dry skin isn't a crisis, those cracks and cuts can open the way to infection. In most cases, some regular moisturising will do the trick, but beware of any wounds that won't heal – they could be a sign of a more serious illness like diabetes.

- Peeling and itching – Dry skin can also be a symptom of a fungal infection like the dreaded athlete's foot, especially when accompanied by peeling, itching, scaling and inflammation. Fungus often shows up in the warm, moist area between the toes where it can easily spread to the nails if left untreated. Fungus can be easy to pick up, especially if you like to go

'The Ancient Greek philosopher Socrates once claimed, "When our feet hurt, we hurt all over".'

barefoot on the beach or in the changing room. Your best defence is to keep your feet protected with footwear and keep your feet dry with fresh socks and talcum powder as needed.

- Thick, yellow nails – It could be the normal effects of ageing, but it could also be a sign of nail fungus. Embarrassment aside, fungus can be difficult to treat because topical medications like creams often aren't effective and oral medications can have potentially harmful side effects, like liver damage.

- Black or dark toenails – Often the result of an injury, the colour is caused by a bruise under the nail. Unfortunately, the bruise can lead to other problems like a fungal infection or a sore that could become infected. Discoloured nails should be checked out, especially if you have diabetes.

- Ingrown toenails – Improper grooming techniques, injury, hereditary and structural problems can all cause the toenail to curl under and dig painfully into the skin. Poorly fitting shoes are also a cause, so it's no surprise this problem shows up more often in women than men. Luckily, it can be treated by a podiatrist.

- Pain – There's one rule when it comes to pain: 'Don't ignore it; it's not normal,' says Dr. Nadal. Foot pain can have many causes, from arthritis to plantar fasciitis, but you'll need some expert advice to determine the problem and find a treatment. Osteoarthritis is a common problem, but it's not the only cause. Pain and inflammation could also be due to a systemic condition like rheumatoid arthritis. Injury and repetitive stress can also cause tendonitis. A proper diagnosis is important.

- Heel pain – Arch and heel pain could be a 'mechanical problem' – that is, the parts of your feet (like your joints and tendons) aren't balanced properly. Not only can this cause pain in your feet, it can also impact on your knees, hips and back, and even contribute to neck pain.

- Pain in the toe – Think it's just a sprain? The big toe is a popular site for attacks of gout, a form of arthritis where a build-up of uric acid in the body can deposit and crystallise in the sacks that surround joints. The sudden onset of pain, swelling and redness can be mistaken for injury, and gout is often diagnosed only after it's happened a few times. If you experience these symptoms, take notes to help your diagnosis.

- Swelling of the ankles – Known medically as 'peripheral oedema', painless swelling in the feet, ankles and legs should warrant a call to your doctor rather than a podiatrist. Sometimes swelling appears because there's too much fluid in the body and it builds up in the extremities. The causes can be quite serious – including heart or kidney failure or a blood clot. If it's accompanied by other strange symptoms like chest pain or shortness of breath, a trip to the doctor or accident and emergency is in order.

However, swelling could also be a side effect of certain medications like hormone treatments or blood pressure medications.

- Tingling or numbness – We've all experienced that feeling of our feet 'being asleep', but regular numbness or tingling could be a sign of nerve or circulatory issues. While vitamin deficiencies, autoimmune disorders and certain medications could be behind it, many people with diabetes experience poor circulation as well as problems with the nerves. Numbness should never go unaddressed because it can mask painful problems like foot ulcers and bone conditions that can get worse quite quickly. The message here? Be extra vigilant and inspect your feet regularly.

- Foot deformities – Whether due to heredity, injury or illness, foot deformities like hammer toes and bunions can be painful to endure.

- Unusual growths – Yes, cancer can occur in the feet too, so any usual growths or lesions should be looked at. However, a more common condition that occurs between the fourth and fifth toe is called 'neuroma', an enlarged (but benign) growth of nerves. Pressure from ill-fitting shoes and bone structure issues is often the cause, and corrective footwear is often a good way to counter it.

'Numbness should never go unaddressed because it can mask painful problems like foot ulcers and bone conditions that can get worse quite quickly.'

10 tips to keep your feet healthy

'Healthy feet are important for feeling good and staying active. So if you neglect your feet, it can lead to unnecessary pain and other foot problems,' says Elizabeth Kurtz, DPM, a podiatrist in Chicago and spokesperson for the American Podiatric Medical Association (APMA).

Fortunately, it's easy to keep your feet healthy. Use these tips to keep yourself active and your feet pain-free:

1. Keep your feet clean and dry. Healthy feet start with good hygiene. Thoroughly clean and scrub your feet with soap and water when you bathe. Afterward, dry them well. Fungal organisms love moisture, so depriving them of any wetness will make it more difficult for them to thrive. Be sure to dry well between each individual toe, any excess moisture between the toes can create a great environment for a fungal infection to begin.

2. Examine your feet for problems. Perform a foot self-exam once a week when you take a bath or shower, as you're drying off your feet, take a good look on the soles for any scaling and between your toes for peeling areas. That could signal athlete's foot. Also look for discolouration of the nails, which could indicate a nail fungus. If you have diabetes, you should inspect your feet every day since diabetes leads to higher risk of foot sores and infections.

3. Cut toenails properly. Cut nails straight across and avoid trimming too close to the skin or drastically rounding the corners of the nails, which can cause painful, ingrown toenails.

4. Don't hide 'ugly' toenails with polish. A discoloured, thick, cracked or crumbling nail could signal a nail fungus. Applying nail polish to an infected nail could make the problem worse.

5. Protect your feet in public areas. Be sure to wear shower shoes at the gym, in changing rooms, and at public pools. These places tend to be breeding grounds for fungi that can lead to infections.

6. Avoid sharing footwear. You can get fungal infections by wearing other people's shoes, as well as socks worn by another person. Always wear your own footwear to help keep your feet healthy.

7. Your feet have sweat glands galore – 250,000 in each foot! Perspiration creates the perfect environment for bacteria to set up shop. Wearing socks that keep feet dry will help your feet stay healthy. Socks made of synthetic fibres tend to wick away moisture faster than cotton or wool socks. Also avoid wearing excessively tight stockings or tights, which trap moisture.

8. Choose breathable footwear. To help keep your feet dry and healthy, wear shoes made of leather to allow air to circulate. If you're prone to excessively sweaty feet, look for shoes made of mesh fabrics for maximum breathability.

'Keep your feet clean and dry. Healthy feet start with good hygiene.'

Need2Know

9. Wear shoes that fit properly. Shoes that are too tight can cause long-term foot problems. Shop for shoes at the end of the day to compensate for foot swelling that occurs later in the day, and wear the same type of socks or hosiery you'll be wearing with the shoes. Choose a broad, rounded shoe with plenty of room for your toes and a wide, stable heel. Avoid pointy shoes, which can cramp your toes and cause ingrown toenails and calluses.

10. Know when to see a doctor. Don't attempt to self-treat painful foot woes. Any pain, redness, swelling, or discolouration that persists should be checked out by a podiatric physician. Usually the problem can be cleared up with prescription medicine or a minor clinic procedure. Allowing a doctor to take a look will help prevent minor problems from becoming major ones.

Seasonal foot care

As the seasons change so do the conditions that our feet suffer, so make sure your feet look great for the seasons all year round. Summertime is a great time to let our feet breathe with summer footwear. Use these ten summer foot care tips from The Society of Chiropodists and Podiatrists to get your feet in shape for summer.

1. Trim your toenails for summer. Use proper nail clippers and cut straight across, not too short, and not down at the corners as this can lead to ingrown nails. File them, if that's easier.

2. Go barefoot. Go barefoot or wear open-toed sandals whenever you can in the hot weather (except when you're in a communal shower or changing area) to help stop your feet getting sweaty and smelly.

3. Forget flip-flops. Don't be tempted to wear flip-flops all through the summer. They don't provide support for your feet and can give you arch and heel pain if you wear them for too long.

4. Change socks daily. If you have to wear socks in hot weather, change them once a day and choose ones that contain at least 70% cotton or wool to keep your feet dry and stop them smelling.

'Don't be tempted to wear flip-flops all through the summer. They don't provide support for your feet and can give you arch and heel pain if you wear them for too long.'

5. Remove hard skin. Hard, cracked skin around the heels is very common in summer, often caused by open-backed sandals and flip-flops rubbing around the edge of the heel. Use a foot file, emery board or pumice stone to gently rub away the hard skin, then apply a rich moisturising cream such as aqueous cream or E45 to soften the skin.

6. Banish blisters. Blisters strike more often in hot weather. They're caused by rubbing, especially between the toes if you're wearing flip-flops with 'thongs' that fit between the toes. Lorraine Jones, a podiatrist from The Society of Chiropodists and Podiatrists, says the key to preventing summer blisters is to keep your feet dry, wear shoes or sandals that fit well and aren't too loose, and give your feet ample rest so they don't get hot and sweaty. If you do get a blister, don't put a plaster over it. Leave it to dry out on its own.

'If you have any problems, such as hard skin that you can't get rid of, it's best to seek professional help.'

7. Ring the changes. Wear a variety of different sandals and shoes during summer to help prevent cracked heels, hard skin and blisters. Lorraine says: 'We understand that when the summer arrives, people are naturally going to opt for lightweight footwear such as flip-flops and flimsy sandals. However, we'd recommend alternating your footwear so that you aren't wearing this style of shoe day in and day out.'

8. Watch out for foot infections. The floors of communal showers and changing rooms at open-air and hotel swimming pools are hot spots for infections such as athlete's foot and verrucas. Don't wander around public pools barefoot. Protect your feet by wearing flip-flops in the changing room and at the pool edge.

9. Tackle sweat. If you have sweaty feet in the summer, it's even more important to wash your feet each morning and evening in warm, soapy water then dry them thoroughly. You can also use an antibacterial wash, which helps deal with foot odour. Then wipe them with cotton wool dipped in surgical spirit and dust them with talc.

10. Get help if you need it. Basic hygiene and nail cutting should be all you need to keep your feet healthy. But if you have any problems, such as hard skin that you can't get rid of, it's best to seek professional help. Your GP will be able to advise you on local foot services.

Registered podiatrists (also known as chiropodists) are trained in all aspects of care for the feet.

You may be able to get NHS treatment from a podiatrist or chiropodist. Some NHS podiatry services offer self-referral, so you don't have to go through your GP.

Summing Up

- The condition of your feet reflect the overall condition of your health and wellbeing.

- Common syptoms of foot problems include: dry/cracked skin, peeling and itching, ingrown toenails, heel pain and swelling, to name just a few.

- If you experience these or any other symptoms mentioned, consult your doctor or a podiatrist.

- Taking good care of your feet on a daily basis all year round by following the tips given in this chapter will help ensure your feet stay healthy and problem free.

Chapter Four

Where to Find Professional Help for Foot Problems

There are several healthcare professionals that can help you if you are suffering from problems with your feet. Your general practitioner (GP) is the best person to contact initially if you think you have a foot problem. Your GP will examine your feet and make an assessment as to whether he or she can give you medication and treatment for your condition, or whether you need further expert help and assistance. Following is a detailed guide to health experts you can consult for help with foot concerns and problems.

'There is no difference between a chiropodist and a podiatrist.'

A general practitioner (GP)

A GP is a medical practitioner who treats acute and chronic illnesses and provides preventive care and health education for all ages and both sexes. They have particular skills in treating people with multiple health issues.

Chiropodist and podiatrist

There is no difference between a chiropodist and a podiatrist.

Chiropodists and podiatrists are autonomous healthcare professionals who aim to improve the mobility, independence and quality of life for their patients. They assess, diagnose and treat people with problems of the feet, ankles and lower limbs.

A chiropodist or a podiatrist can work independently or as part of a multidisciplinary team. Most practitioners start their professional careers working in general clinics, then specialise in rheumatology, diabetes, dermatology, wound care, biomechanics or sports injuries.

As a registered practitioner in the NHS, they may work in a hospital or the community, including: an outpatient clinic or surgery room, a hospital ward or GPs' surgery, and in people's homes. Chiropodists and podiatrists can also undergo further training to become a podiatric surgeon, or forensic podiatrist.

Podiatric surgeon

Podiatric surgeons should not be confused with orthopaedic surgeons.

Podiatric surgeons have trained exclusively for 10 years in the surgical and non-surgical treatment of the foot. Orthopaedic surgeons complete a medicine degree before going on to further training in the management of bone and joint conditions which affect the whole body.

Podiatric surgery training begins with the non-surgical management of foot problems and then after completing a three-year degree and at least one post-registration year in clinical practice, surgical training can commence and takes a further 6 years.

Although podiatric surgeons specialise in the foot as part of their training, they understand other medical conditions and diseases which may not originate in the foot but may give rise to symptoms there.

The advantage of such a focused training and scope of practice is that a podiatric surgeon will gain intensive experience in managing foot problems.

Their wide scope of practice on the foot enables them to develop highly skilled and meticulous surgical techniques, as well as great experience in handling complications which are unfortunately an inevitable part of any surgery speciality.

Orthopaedic surgeon

An orthopaedic surgeon is a medical doctor with extensive postgraduate training in the proper diagnosis and treatment of injuries and diseases of the musculoskeletal system.

Orthopaedics is a medical specialty devoted to the diagnosis, treatment, rehabilitation and prevention of injuries and diseases of the musculoskeletal system. This includes bones, joints, ligaments, tendons, muscles and nerves; and could be anything from a broken finger to a hip replacement, repairing damaged tendons or delicate spinal surgery.

The specialty of orthopaedic surgery is devoted to the care of all ages, from newborns with birth defects through to senior citizens with arthritis and fractures. Sports injuries are also an important part of orthopaedic surgery.

People often think that orthopaedic surgeons just do operations. This is not the case. A large part of orthopaedic practice is the non-operative management of musculoskeletal conditions.

Orthopaedic treatments are becoming more varied every year and there are now specialists within this specialty. This means your GP could refer you to a 'hand' specialist or a 'hip' specialist, for example.

'The specialty of orthopaedic surgery is devoted to the care of all ages, from newborns with birth defects through to senior citizens with arthritis and fractures.'

Physiotherapist

A physiotherapist is a healthcare professional who specialises in maximising human movement, function and potential.

A physiotherapist may work with someone after injury, accident or surgery, or may work to prevent injury, for instance with sporting clubs or in the workplace.

Physiotherapists work in a wide variety of settings: hospitals, private clinics, hospices, nursing homes, a patient's own home, the workplace, sports clubs and gyms.

Physiotherapy is available on the NHS. Your family GP can refer you for physiotherapy. Some areas operate an open access system so you can refer yourself for physiotherapy assessment.

Foot injuries commonly occur during sporting activities such as running and jumping. Conditions that affect the foot can be caused by direct injury, repetitive overuse or poor foot posture, such as flat footedness. Physiotherapy can help to address and correct some of these issues.

Prosthetist and orthotist

Prosthetists and orthotists provide care for anyone requiring an artificial limb (prosthesis) or a device to support or control part of the body (orthosis). They will also advise on rehabilitation.

Orthotists provide a range of splints, braces and special footwear to aid movement, correct deformity and relieve discomfort.

Prosthetists provide the best possible artificial replacement for patients who have lost or were born without a limb. A prosthetic limb should feel and look like a natural limb.

'Foot injuries commonly occur during sporting activities such as running and jumping.'

Tips on choosing a foot care specialist

Choosing a foot specialist to care for your feet is just like choosing your family doctor or dentist. You want someone you can trust, someone who is fully qualified and up to date with all the latest techniques and someone who will help you to get well and stay well.

When choosing a specialist:

- Ask friends and family for a recommendation.
- Ask your doctor or healthcare provider for a recommendation.
- Contact your Podiatry Association in your city or town. They can help you to choose a foot specialist within your locality who can help assist you with your foot problem.
- Most Podiatrists are listed under 'P' in the yellow pages.

A few extra tips . . .

Most foot doctors have areas of special interest. For this reason it is worth asking your foot specialist what area they prefer to specialise in. Naturally, a foot specialist who prefers to specialise in the treatment of ingrown toenails is the best person to treat your ingrown toenails.

It has been estimated that the feet travel anywhere from 5,000 to 12,000 steps per day on average. This means your feet are your main form of transport. We only get one pair so it's worth looking after them.

Online resources to find professionals

Resources such as www.bookmyfeet.com offer a nationwide network of podiatrists, chiropodists and foot health professionals, providing foot care treatments locally to you.

Online websites such as these can offer home and surgery visits nationwide.

Take time to browse these websites, some of the information put together is to help you, the patient, understand the services and treatments offered throughout the UK. Many of these websites also have great foot care advice information pages where you will find information from general care to more complex problems.

Websites such as www.drfoot.co.uk also have useful resources to help identify foot problems with their online 'Foot Pain Identifier'.

Although websites can be a very useful resource for information, please remember that nothing can substitute the advice and information of a professional foot care expert, so always contact a medical or expert professional for peace of mind and reassurance.

Chiropody and costs

Chiropodists, also sometimes known as podiatrists, treat a wide variety of abnormalities and conditions of the foot and lower limb, from verrucas and ingrown toenails, to arthritis.

Chiropodists work with people of all ages, but also play an important role in helping older people and disabled people to stay mobile and independent.

Chiropody is available on the NHS free of charge in most areas of the UK, although the availability in your local area will depend on your Primary Care Trust (PCT).

Each case is also assessed on an individual basis. Whether or not you receive free treatment will depend on how serious your condition is and how quickly it needs to be treated. If your condition is unlikely to affect your health, or mobility, you may not be eligible for treatment.

People with diabetes

Most people with diabetes who need to see a chiropodist are treated as priority cases, although some PCTs will only prioritise people if their diabetes is severe. Your PCT will be able to provide you with more information about their referral policies.

Referral

To have treatment with a chiropodist, you will need a referral from your GP, practice nurse or health visitor.

If treatment is available in your area, your case will be assessed, and you will be added to a waiting list. If necessary, it may be possible to arrange a chiropodist to come out to your home. Tell your GP if you will need to have a home visit.

Private treatment

If free NHS treatment is not available in your area, your GP can still refer you to a local clinic for private treatment, but you will have to pay.

If you decide to contact a chiropodist yourself, make sure that they are fully qualified, registered with the Health Professionals Council (HPC) and that they are an accredited member of one of the following organisations:

- The British Chiropody and Podiatry Association.
- The Society of Chiropodists and Podiatrists.
- The Institute of Chiropodists and Podiatrists.

Summing Up

- The foot is more complex than a lot of people realise. It is complex enough to have its own medical specialty.

- There are numerous professionals you can seek help from for foot problems, including: chiropodists and podiatrists, orthopaedic surgeons and physiotherapists, as well as your GP.

- Podiatry (healthcare of the foot and leg) may seem like a strange specialty, but in reality there are many conditions in which seeing a podiatrist, or 'foot doctor' would be preferred over seeing any other type of medical technician or doctor.

- Common foot and leg ailments and related minor injuries can be and are often treated by a general practitioner.

- If you have a more complex injury or are active in sports or work that requires full health of your feet and legs then seeing a specialist in podiatry is probably the best option for you.

- If you decide to contact a chiropodist yourself, make sure that they are fully qualified and registered with the Health Professionals Council (HPC)

- If free NHS treatment is not available in your area, your GP can still refer you to a local clinic for private treatment, but you will have to pay.

Chapter Five

Taking Care of Your Feet: Hygiene

On a daily basis, our feet take a good thrashing. Good foot hygiene is important in maintaining healthy feet. Good foot hygiene is also important in preventing foot complications.

To keep your feet healthy, follow these daily tips:

- Wash your feet every day. Use warm, not hot, soapy water. Use a mild, non-perfumed soap, the milder the better, to avoid drying out skin.

- After rinsing your feet, dry them thoroughly. Don't forget to dry between your toes.

- If you have dry skin, apply a mild moisturiser.

- Apply a thin layer of medicated foot powder to the bottoms of your feet to help with perspiration and prevent infection.

- Look for foot problems like cuts, corns, calluses, blisters, ingrown toenails, swelling, discolouration and/or pain. Report any concerns to your general practitioner.

'Good foot hygiene is important in maintaining healthy feet. Good foot hygiene is also important in preventing foot complications.'

Socks and footwear

Cotton socks should be worn instead of synthetic fibres as these allow the feet to breathe and remain cool, and footwear should be altered daily to prevent bacteria from building up.

Toenails

Healthy toenails are a part of good foot hygiene. When trimming your toenails, cut your nails straight across, rounding off outer edges slightly with file i.e. no right angles or sharp corners. Use sharp nail scissors or nail clippers. Soak your nails in warm water before clipping. Also, don't clip your cuticles. The cuticle forms a seal between the top of the nail and the skin, blocking entrance by bacteria. When cuticles are clipped or removed, the lack of protection can lead to infection.

Purchasing foot hygiene products

A variety of quality foot care products, including soaps, deodorants, lotions, powders and nail care items, are available over the counter and by prescription. If you're unsure of the best products to use, talk to your doctor. He or she can recommend products that will work for you.

Natural ways to take care of your feet

Tips and advice on foot care at home

The key to family foot care at home is quite simply that if you give, you shall receive.

There is a home foot care product available in your local pharmacy or to buy online for just about every foot symptom out there. It means that taking care of your feet at home is easier than ever. The trick is to find what works for you.

A little everyday foot pampering may take a bit of time but it feels great. So go ahead and commit yourself to looking at your feet a bit more often and treating them nicely.

If you can't find the time, then make the time. Because just 10 minutes of home foot care each evening of cleaning and filing, followed by lotion and socks will keep your feet looking their best.

Make your home foot care really easy by buying yourself your own home foot bath. This portable unit can be used anywhere in the home, and within minutes will soak and soften the skin on your feet. Add one or two drops of your favourite scented bath lotion and be ready with some warm, soft towels to wrap your feet in when you step out.

Make home foot care part of your daily routine. Be nice to them, and in return you will always have feet to be proud of. You will never have to worry how they look if you want to slip off your socks and shoes at a moment's notice again.

Natural spa pedicures

It is worth spending some time in preparation of natural, home-made foot care recipes during the winter so the summers can be spent in maintaining wonderful soft feet instead of trying to repair the damage. Although emphasis here is on the winter months, it is a good idea to continually give your feet some attention.

The great thing about these recipes is that they go a long way. You only need a couple of minutes to prepare some of them, foot soak or foot scrub recipes for example. The ingredients are those found elsewhere in skin care recipe preparation; simple ingredients such as essential oils, sugar, sea salt . . . all of them easily found and affordable.

For best results, it is advised to stick to a certain order when applying these recipes. The first one is a foot soak, also known as foot bath, which softens the skin making it easier to scrub off dead skin cells. It prepares the feet for a foot scrub. Not only that, they are a great pampering experience. You can adjust the essential oils for the effect you want: relaxation, energy, etc. and enjoy yourself while your feet get a royal treatment.

Make it a point to apply a good cream or moisturiser on them every night. For best results, slather as much as you want and put socks on. Leaving them overnight will do wonders for your feet.

Feet are vulnerable to all kinds of conditions and infections. Anything from athlete's foot, warts and foot corns can affect them, but the good thing is these can all be treated with natural, safe skin remedies.

'Make home foot care part of your daily routine. Be nice to them, and in return you will always have feet to be proud of.'

Baking soda home-made cleanse

Ingredients

½ cup of rice

Water

3 tablespoons of baking soda

Preparation

Cook the rice in enough water so you have rice water left, around 2-3 cups.

Add baking soda into it, let it cool down a bit and dip your feet for as long as the water is warm.

Dry them well.

This simple recipe is very effective for smelly feet, as baking soda acts as an antibacterial agent preventing excessive perspiration. It kills the existing bacteria and prevents any possible infections. The rice water is good for improving microcirculation.

To make it into a tea tree oil foot soak, try adding a couple of drops of tea tree essential oil into it. Tea tree oil is one of the best ingredients to use in order to fight fungal infections such as athlete's foot.

Chopping some parsley into it also has an antibacterial effect and helps improve the circulation.

Salt foot bath

Ingredients

½ cup of sea salt

Water

Preparation

Prepare a large pan of water. Boil it and let it cool down to a temperature you feel comfortable with.

Add the salt into it, let it dissolve and soak your feet.

Salt helps tired, swollen and achey feet. A solution containing salt and water is hypertonic compared to your skin and skin cells. This means that it drains excess water out of your feet and soaks it up.

Lavender herbal foot bath

Ingredients

5 litres of water

2 drops of lavender essential oil

¼ cup of sea salt or Epsom salt

Preparation

Boil the water and let it cool down a bit.

Add the lavender oil and salt.

Immerse your feet.

Lavender is not only used in relaxing bubble baths and foot massage, it is a wonderful ingredient for your feet. It smells good and provides relaxation your feet need.

You could also try sandalwood or ylang-ylang oils, they also have a soothing effect.

Peppermint foot soak recipe

Ingredients

Water (enough to cover your feet and reach your ankles)

3 drops of peppermint essential oil

1 drop of eucalyptus essential oil and 1 drop of lemon essential oil (these two are optional but aid the invigorating sensation of this recipe

Preparation

Boil the water and let it cool down a bit.

Add the oils and keep the feet in as long as you like.

Milky softness

Ingredients

¼ cup of fresh lemon juice

A bit of cinnamon

2 tablespoons of olive oil

¼ cup of milk

¼ cup of water

Preparation

Mix all the ingredients and submerge your feet as long as you like.

For best results, use it twice a week.

After you are done, your skin will feel smooth and pedicure will be a breeze. Cuticle care is performed after this, as they are softened and can be pushed back painlessly.

Foot soak combined with reflexology or foot massage is a great way to relax or rejuvenate your feet. You can combine oils, ingredients, and find a home-made foot soak that is perfect for you.

'Foot soak combined with reflexology or foot massage is a great way to relax or rejuvenate your feet. You can combine oils, ingredients, and find a home-made foot soak that is perfect for you.'

Summing Up

- Employing good hygiene practices will help to prevent many ailments of the foot and nail.

- Athlete's foot and fungal nail infections are very common and can be easily avoided and treated by using some common sense and good cleansing routines.

- Ingrowing toenails can be very painful and can be avoided by making sure the nails are trimmed in the correct way.

- If you are unsure or have difficulty in reaching your toenails, it is advisable to consult a Health Professional Council (HPC) registered podiatrist/ chiropodist.

- Good hygiene practices will help to keep feet in good condition and will aid the prevention of many of the common foot complaints.

- Knowing that your feet look and smell good will also help give you confidence and help feel better about yourself

Chapter Six

Foot Care and Footwear

A survey carried out in 2009 by the Society of Chiropodists and Podiatrists found that 37% of women and 17% of men buy shoes in the sales knowing they're the wrong size.

If your feet are a pain in your life – take a look at the shoes that you are wearing. Do you spend your days wearing high heels on your feet? Do your shoes really fit properly? When was the last time you had your feet measured before you bought a new pair of shoes? High-heeled shoes or improperly fitted shoes cause health problems such as bunions, heel pain and deformed toes, as well as nerve damage.

Your feet are often a good indication of your general health. Not only does wearing improper shoes hurt your feet, knee problems can also result from wearing such shoes.

According to the American Orthopaedic Foot and Ankle Society, women should wear shoes with a height of no more than two and a quarter inches and that even shoes at these heights should be worn no more than two or three hours each day. Wearing heels frequently for long periods of time can shorten the Achilles tendon over time and causes a loss in the range of motion in your feet and ankle.

'High-heeled shoes or improperly fitted shoes cause health problems such as bunions, heel pain and deformed toes, as well as nerve damage.'

Buying shoes that fit

Selecting properly fitting shoes is the first step to eliminating foot pain and preventing possible foot problems. Don't pick your shoes because the tag says they are your size, try them on and buy them based on how they fit on your foot. If you haven't had your feet measured in five years or more, you should get them measured the next time before you buy shoes; feet can change size and shape over the years. And don't measure just one foot, measure both feet. Your feet may be different sizes and you should buy your shoes to fit the larger foot.

Buy your shoes late in the day when your feet may be slightly larger. If your shoes fit properly, there will be ⅜" to ½" of space between the end of your longest toe and the tip of your shoe when you are standing up. Don't expect a tight pair of shoes to stretch to fit your foot, if you do you are asking for foot pain later on. Shoes should have rounded toes that allow your toes room to 'wiggle'.

Remember, when it comes to shoes – 'you are what you wear'.

Pronation and supination

Learn how to identify pronation and supination and then choose the right shoes to support your foot type.

Pronation and supination are two terms that refer to a foot's natural rolling movement while walking or running. This motion is sometimes called the 'walking gait' which is a unique set of actions and reactions that your foot performs while in motion to support, cushion and balance your body. See a qualified podiatrist for a complete foot-strike and walking gait analysis. They will be able to tell you if there are any concerns regarding the way your walking gait is functioning.

What is pronation?

Pronation refers to the inward roll of the foot during normal motion and occurs as the outer edge of the heel strikes the ground and the foot rolls inward and flattens out. A moderate amount of pronation is required for the foot to function properly, however damage and injury can occur during excessive pronation. When excessive pronation does occur the foot arch flattens out and stretches the muscles, tendons and ligaments underneath the foot.

What is supination?

Supination is the opposite of pronation and refers to the outward roll of the foot during normal motion. A natural amount of supination occurs during the push-off phase of the running gait as the heel lifts off the ground and the forefoot and toes are used to propel the body forward. However, excessive supination (outward rolling) places a large strain on the muscles and tendons that stabilise the ankle, and can lead to the ankle rolling completely over, resulting in an ankle sprain or total ligament rupture.

Symptoms

Excessive pronation and supination can cause a number of problems that affect the foot, ankle, knees, hips and back. Some of the more common symptoms of excessive pronation and supination are:

- Arch pain.
- Heel pain.
- Flat feet.
- Corns and calluses.
- Ankle sprains.
- Shin splints.
- Achilles tendonitis.
- Knee pain.
- Hip pain.
- Back pain.

'Pronation and supination are two terms that refer to a foots natural rolling movement while walking or running.'

Summing Up

- One general recommendation that will ease the discomfort of most common foot problems is proper fitting shoes.

- Poorly fitting shoes can make symptoms of foot pain worse and in many cases be the primary cause of the problem. It is important to purchase footwear that fits properly from the moment you buy them.

- Never buy footwear hoping they will 'break in' later.

- Properly fitted shoes allow adequate room to freely wiggle your toes. Poorly fitting shoes can also cause or aggravate bunions, calluses, hammer toes, and other common foot problems. For many people with more serious conditions like diabetes, proper fitting footwear is even more critical.

- There are many things to consider when purchasing new footwear. The fit and support of the footwear are the two most important.

- A good tip to remember is to buy shoes late in the day when your feet may be slightly larger.

- You can benefit from having your feet measured and professionally fitted by experts who understand the way footwear is supposed to fit.

- Pronation and supination are biomechanical problems, and are best treated and prevented with orthotic inserts.

- Pronation refers to the inward roll of the foot during normal motion and occurs as the outer edge of the heel strikes the ground.

- Supination is the opposite of pronation and refers to the outward roll of the foot during normal motion.

- Before you run out to buy orthotics it makes sense to get the right advice on footwear.

- Good quality footwear will go a long way in helping to prevent pronation and supination.

Chapter Seven

Foot Health: Exercise, Diet and Nutrition

Like the rest of your body, your feet need exercise to stay in great shape. Podiatric surgeon Jacqueline Sutera, suggests some simple basic exercises to keep your feet healthy.

Foot exercises

- Toe grip – Toe grip is a good exercise to strengthen the foot muscles to improve balance. Drop a sock on the floor and use your toes to grip and lift it off the floor. Hold for 10 seconds, then release. Repeat five times with each foot.

- Toe extension – Toe extension is a good way to strengthen and support the muscles, which in turn will protect the bones of the feet: Wrap an elastic band around all five toes. Expand your toes and hold for five seconds; release. Repeat five times on each foot.

- Calf raise – Calf raise exercises are good to strengthen the feet and the calves and improve balance. Stand near a counter or a doorway and hold on lightly for balance. Balance on one foot and rise up onto your toes. Hold for 10 seconds, and then lower. Repeat 10 times on each foot.

- Calf stretch – Calf stretch exercises keep the Achilles tendons and the plantar fasciae from getting tight. Sit with one leg stretched out in front of you and wrap a towel around the ball of the foot. Pull the towel back gently until you feel a stretch in the arch of the foot and the calf. Hold for 10 seconds then release. Repeat five times on each leg.

'Like the rest of your body, your feet need exercise to stay in great shape.'

Walking

Walking is a great simple exercise you can do to maintain healthy, beautiful feet. It stimulates the circulation to your feet and keeps them healthy and strong. Be sure to wear suitable shoes.

'Walking stimulates the circulation to your feet and keeps them healthy and strong. Be sure to wear suitable shoes.'

Diet and nutrition

When most people think about nutrition and their health, they normally associate the foods they eat with weight loss or heart health. However, your diet affects many other parts of your body, including your feet.

Your feet are connected to the rest of your body, and what you put into your body is what makes up how you body feels, that includes your feet.

Feet and nutrition

Fighting off inflammation and pain

One problem linked to nutrition that can affect your feet is inflammation. Certain foods can increase chemicals in your body that cause tissue inflammation. This inflammation could appear in your foot as 'plantar fasciitis', which causes pain in the thick band of tissue that runs across the bottom of your foot, in your heel, or elsewhere in your foot.

Many common foods in the British diet encourage inflammation, such as the refined grains, sugar and trans fats in many baked goods and junk foods; the saturated fat in red meat and the omega-6 fats found in many commonly used vegetable oils, such as corn, soybean and sunflower oils.

In addition, some people may have increased levels of inflammation in their bodies due to chronic allergies to common foods such as wheat. Another factor that can contribute to inflammation is eating too many foods that cause your blood sugar to rise quickly, such as sweets, white flour and pasta.

Reducing inflammation of the feet

You can help reduce inflammation by eating more omega-3 fats. Fatty fish such as salmon, as well as fish oil supplements, are good sources of omega-3s.

Omega-3s help reduce inflammation, and nutrition studies suggest they should be properly balanced in the diet with omega-6s. Most people's diets provide far more omega-6s than omega-3s, and a fish-rich diet can address this imbalance.

'One problem linked to nutrition that can affect your feet is inflammation.'

A healthy lifestyle

Following an overall healthier diet can provide anti-inflammatory benefits to your feet and your total health. This includes eating more green vegetables and other fresh plant foods, and cutting out refined grain foods and sugary treats.

Feet and nutrition: other health connections

Two common conditions that affect millions of people's feet are peripheral artery disease and diabetes. Each of these conditions can harm your feet by damaging arteries that bring blood to your lower extremities.

Good nutrition can also help protect your feet from these conditions. According to the National Institutes of Health (NIH), a diet low in saturated fat, trans fat and sodium, and rich in fruits and vegetables can help reduce your risk of artery disease.

Diabetes

If you have diabetes, a healthy diet can help protect your feet from complications of that condition too. In general, a diet rich in wholegrains, beans, vegetables and fruits, lean meats, and a limited amount of fats and sweets is recommended by healthcare professionals.

Cramps

'Your feet may be one of the first places to see the effects of osteoporosis.'

Another common condition which some experience are foot or leg cramps. It is believed that many times these are caused by nutritional deficiencies. The best way to avoid cramps related to nutrition is to eat a healthy, balanced diet packed with essential nutrients. The most common deficiencies related to cramps indicate a possible lack of potassium or vitamin D.

Dehydration, a lack of water in the muscles, can also make you prone to cramping in your feet or legs. Keeping yourself hydrated, especially when exercising, is the best remedy for cramps resulting from dehydration. Alcohol consumption increases your odds for dehydration, so be careful with your alcohol use. Smoking is a big culprit also and it is best not to smoke at all.

Osteoporosis

Your feet may be one of the first places to see the effects of osteoporosis. A stress fracture in the foot is often the first sign. There is a lot you can do throughout your life to prevent osteoporosis, slow its progression and protect yourself from fractures. Include adequate amounts of calcium and vitamin D in your diet and exercise regularly.

Whether you eat more health-conciously to counteract a medical condition or to avoid one, following the recommendations to eat healthily will help ensure that your feet, along with the rest of your body, continue to serve you well. Consult your GP or a nutritional expert for further information about feet and nutrition.

Summing Up

▓ Due to the nature of their work, there are hundreds of things that can go wrong with the feet.

▓ Some of the more common foot ailments are orthopaedic problems such as flat feet and tendonitis; injuries, such as stress fractures; and simple degeneration from age and overuse.

▓ The good thing is, the feet are amazingly resilient and flexible and, often, foot problems can be resolved with simple stretches and conditioning exercises.

▓ To prevent injury to your feet consult your GP or foot care specialist for further advice on foot exercises.

▓ Following the NIH's recommendations for healthy eating will help ensure that your feet, along with the rest of your body, continue to serve you well.

▓ Following an overall healthier diet can provide anti-inflammatory benefits to your feet and your total health. This includes eating more green vegetables and other fresh plant foods, and cutting out refined grain foods and sugary treats.

▓ Eat more omega-3 fats. Fatty fish such as salmon, as well as fish oil supplements, are good sources of omega-3s.

▓ Another factor that can contribute to inflammation of the feet is eating too many foods that cause your blood sugar to rise quickly, such as sweets, white flour and pasta, avoid them if you suffer from swollen feet. Also, diabetics need to be especially vigilant about what they eat.

▓ Your feet may be one of the first places to see the effects of osteoporosis. A stress fracture in the foot is often the first sign.

▓ Consult your GP or a nutritional expert for further information about feet and nutrition.

Family Foot Care: Healthy Feet for the Whole Family – A Guide

Making sure your family have healthy feet all year round will mean no painful foot problems or visits to the doctor later on. And it's probably up to you, if you're a parent reading this, to make good foot care a family thing.

Following these important steps will leave the whole family walking tall:

- Make sure young children are drying their feet well, especially in-between the toes.

- Kids should wear cotton socks. They are absorbent and let air circulate around the feet.

- The younger members of your family need their toenails clipped straight across keeping them short and neatly trimmed.

- Any signs of toenail infections (for example, redness, inflammation or hardness around the edge) should be checked out with your doctor as soon as possible. In the meantime at home a warm compress may work well if the area is painful.

- Be sure to get your child's foot measured each season and check that they are not wearing shoes of the wrong size. Badly fitting shoes can do enormous damage to young growing feet and toes.

- It's not a good idea to share the same shoes amongst different family members. Although it may seem you are constantly buying shoes for your children's growing feet, each child moulds a shoe to the exact shape of their foot while wearing them. Shoes passed down in the family could potentially damage the next child's feet.

- On the whole, men don't pay as much attention to their own foot care as women do. But that's not to say they shouldn't. Apart from using nail clippers, most men don't own their own set of pedicure tools. But it does seem these days that men are opting for the occasional professional pedicure more than ever before.

- The rules for foot care are the same for men as they are for woman: cleanse, file, exfoliate and moisturise. There is a fantastic range of good-looking products around such as sea sponges and long-handled hard skin files that can be used on feet while in the shower.

- Keep a basket of fun products by the side of the bath and shower for the family to use to promote family foot care. For example, fresh natural-scented moisturisers will appeal to men, while colourful nail brushes and sponges with funny faces on will entice the youngsters.

- Metal nail files work well on tough toenails and can be cleaned thoroughly in hot soapy water after use for another family member to use. Remember to keep sharp skin and nail tools away from young children at all times.

- If you have a family member who suffers from diabetes, then remember to pay particular attention to their feet.

Foot care should be a family thing. Family foot care is an important part of a personal hygiene routine that will ensure your family enjoy good foot health for the rest of their lives.

Part 2:

Foot Problems Explained

A Comprehensive Guide to Foot Problems,
Their Symptoms, Causes and Treatments

Chapter Eight

The Top 5 Most Common Foot Problems in the UK

Feet are like snowflakes: no two are the same – even those on the same body. Your feet may actually be two different shoe sizes! And even if they're evenly matched, they'll be different sizes and different shapes at different times in your life, including as your body changes through growth, pregnancy, disease or disability, and ageing. Because of these natural irregularities and the changes that every person encounters during life, there are several everyday foot problems that often occur.

Uncomfortable footwear may be a factor behind many everyday foot problems.

Many foot problems are hereditary, including bunions, hammer toes, flat feet, gout, even ingrown toenails. And, although greatly influenced by calcium intake, exercise and hormonal changes, bone strength is partly hereditary. It's also influenced by racial factors. Asian people, for example, have less bone mass than white people, and white people have less bone mass than black people; the greater your bone mass, the less likely you are to develop arthritis or the brittle bones of osteoporosis.

Nationality can also influence foot structure. Many Mediterranean people, for instance, have particularly low arches, while many Northern Europeans tend to have high ones. Finally, in some ethnic communities, cultural standards play a role, because they determine what is considered attractive. Members suffer pain from wearing uncomfortable shoes that are simply de rigueur in their cultural world.

One of your best precautions against foot pain is to be aware of both the hereditary factors (which you can't change) and the lifestyle and life-stage factors (which you can change or, at least, influence) that determine whether your feet are healthy or hurting.

The top five most common foot problems

Hamish Dow is a leading podiatrist and is registered with the Health Professionals Council; active in his local branch of The Society of Chiropodists and Podiatrists, where he is currently vice chairman. He has represented the branch at regional branch level and at its Annual Delegate Assembly.

Hamish Dow has pinpointed the top five most common foot problems in the UK as being:

1. Calluses.

2. Toenail problems.

3. Heel pain.

4. Fungal nail conditions.

5. Warts/Verrucas.

How to identify foot problems

Foot problems can be common with people who are on their feet for hours at a time. In addition, some people do not always exert good judgement when it comes foot care and footwear. Tight shoes and high heels worn for long periods of time can lead to foot problems. A person who is concerned about their feet should consult a podiatrist, but it is possible to identify some of the more common foot problems. Those who suffer from diabetes should take particular care of their feet and should also consult a physician with any problems.

▪ Examine your feet, particularly if you notice red, itchy, flaky skin between your toes. You may be suffering from a fungal condition, commonly known as athlete's foot. This is properly known as tinea pedes and is more common in men and teenagers. Treat this with an antifungal medications. This condition may be spread through the use of communal showers. Consult your doctor or an expert if this problem is causing you concern,

- Look for either a soft, or hard small area of raised white skin if you feel sharp, intense pain in an area of your foot. This may indicate a corn, which is a common foot complaint. Corns are found in the areas of your foot that are subject to pressure. They can usually be treated effectively by over-the-counter treatments that break down the corns. If you feel an intense pain and cannot find an obvious corn, check this with your podiatrist or physician.

- Examine your foot if you are suffering pain around the big toe joint. Look for signs of inflammation. Bunions happen where the big toe becomes angled inward towards the middle of the foot and the second toe. This can force the top of the first metatarsal to protrude from the foot, at the bottom of the big toe, where a painful bunion forms. This is treated with painkillers, special pads and, in severe cases, by surgery.

- Check the joint of your toe to see if the end curls back on itself and if it is becoming rigid. This may be indicative of hammer toe. You may also notice a corn on the end of the toe. Medical attention should be sought if you suspect this condition, as it will not get better on its own. Hammer toe is due to contracture of the joint, possibly triggered by a tendon/muscle imbalance, and is made worse by tight shoes. Early intervention may involve splints, cortisone injections or orthotic devices.

- Check your foot if you suspect a verruca, also known as a plantar wart. This may be situated on the ball of your foot, the bottom of your toe or on your heel. Verrucas may have small black spots near the center and can be painful if weight is put on the area. Verrucas are caused by a strain of papillomavirus and seem to be easily caught if you have a break in the skin. Verrucas may be treated with over-the-counter lotions. If this problem is persistent contact an expert professional in foot care.

- Check your toenails for any discolouration or signs of infection. Any painful sensation around the toenail might indicate infection. You might also notice a brittleness, crumbling and discolouration of the nail itself. This is caused by a fungal infection and should be treated by a podiatrist.

The top 5: causes, symptoms and treatment

Calluses

A callus is caused by an accumulation of dead skin cells that harden and thicken over an area of the foot. This callus formation is the body's defence mechanism to protect the foot against excessive pressure and friction. Calluses are normally found on the ball of the foot, the heel, and/or the inside of the big toe.

What is the cause of a callus?

- Calluses develop because of excessive pressure at a specific area of the foot.
- Some common causes of callus formation are high-heeled shoes or shoes that are too small.
- Obesity can cause friction on one area of the foot causing a callus to form.
- Abnormalities in the walking motion (gait cycle) can cause a callus to form.
- Flat feet.
- High arched feet.
- Excessively long metatarsal bone.
- Bony prominence.
- Loss of fat pad on the underside of the foot.
- Short Achilles tendon.

Symptoms of a foot callus

The most common symptoms are:

- A hard growth usually on the ball of the foot.
- Pain on weight bearing, relieved by rest.

⁙ Increased discomfort in thin-soled and high-heeled shoes.

Treatments for calluses

The most important thing about treating calluses is to *never* attempt to do it yourself because calluses may be a symptom of other foot problems. It is always necessary to have a specialist examine your feet and establish the cause of your condition. Unless the cause of the condition is found and removed, calluses will continue to form.

Beware

Don't ever attempt to cut away or scrape a callus! If you accidentally cut yourself, the warm, moist confines of enclosed shoes will quickly turn small cuts into serious wounds.

Over-the-counter remedies such as corn paint or special plasters only treat the symptoms, and not the problem. Also, inappropriate use of such remedies can result in damaging the healthy skin surrounding the calluses.

If you've got calluses or believe you may be developing them, see a podiatrist for treatment.

Possibilities for treatment will include:

⁙ Isolating and removing the source of the condition (the cause of friction and pressure).

⁙ Prescribing an antibiotic ointment to reduce the risk of an infection.

⁙ Professional reduction of the callus to relieve pain.

⁙ Customised padding to redistribute pressure.

⁙ Advice on appropriate footwear and foot care (perhaps applying a specific moisturiser).

Depending on how developed calluses are the doctor may recommend permanent shoe inserts (orthoses) for long-term pressure relief.

Preventing calluses

- Always wear shoes that fit right; never wear other's shoes.

- Take notice of extra pressure on certain areas of your feet and act immediately to prevent the formation of calluses.

- Using a moisturiser daily will keep your skin supple.

- Wash your feet with soap and water every evening; use a scrubbing brush.

- Treat any foot pain or foot skin irritation as it occurs.

- Change your socks daily and avoid your feet getting sweaty.

- Regularly see a specialist for a foot check-up!

- Avoid walking around barefoot and always wear shoes outside.

- Use special padding to cushion the foot areas where you feel there's additional pressure.

- Soak your feet in a hot water bath with a couple of drops of essential oil, like lavender or eucalyptus, twice or three times a week; after bathing, gently rub off a layer of thickened skin with a washcloth or pumice stone. You should not remove the tough skin all at once!

Ingrown toenails

An ingrown toenail, also known as onychocryptosis or unguis incarnatus, is a painful condition of the toe. It occurs when a sharp corner of the toenail digs into the skin at the end of or side of the toe. Pain and inflammation at the spot where the nail curls into the skin occurs first. Later, the inflamed area can begin to grow extra tissue or drain yellowish fluid.

If left untreated, an ingrown toenail can progress to an infection or even an abscess that requires surgical treatment.

Ingrown toenails are common in adults but uncommon in children and infants. They are more common in men than in women. Young adults in their 20s or 30s are most at risk.

Any toenail can become ingrown, but the condition is usually found in the big toe.

Causes of ingrown toenails

▒ Tight-fitting shoes or high heels cause the toes to be compressed together and pressure the nail to grow abnormally.

▒ Improper trimming of toenails can cause the corners of the nail to dig into the skin. Nails should be trimmed straight across, not rounded.

▒ Disorders such as fungal infections of the nail can cause a thickened or widened toenail to develop.

▒ Either an acute injury near the nail or anything that causes the nail to be damaged repetitively (such as playing soccer) can also cause an ingrown nail.

▒ If a member of your family has an ingrown toenail, then you are more likely to develop one, too. Some people's nails are normally more rounded than others, which increases the chance of developing ingrown nails.

Symptoms of ingrown toenails

An ingrown toenail is a common disorder that most often affects the outer edge of the big toe. However, the nail on any toe, or the nail on both sides of a toe can become ingrown. The most common signs and symptoms are pain, redness and swelling at the corner of a toenail.

Early in the course of an ingrown toenail, the end of the toe becomes reddened and painful with mild swelling. There is no pus or drainage. It may feel warm to the touch, but you will not have a fever.

Later, extra skin and tissue will grow around the sharp point of the nail. A yellowish drainage may begin. This is the body's response to the trauma of a nail irritating the skin and is not necessarily an infection.

Sometimes an infection develops. In this case, the swelling will become worse, and there may be white or yellow-coloured drainage from the area. A lighter coloured area of the skin may be surrounded by red skin. You may develop a fever, although this is unusual.

Treatment of ingrown toenails

A visit to your GP may be in order to assess the condition of your toenails. If no acute infection is found, then the nail will be elevated and conservative treatment recommended. This consists of warm soaks, proper shoes and frequent cleaning of the nail.

Sometimes, your doctor or a foot care specialist will choose to use a splint. Several types of splints can be used. These vary in type, but they all protect the skin from the sharp corner of the nail. Some of the most common types of splints include cotton wicks, plastic strips, plastic tubes down the side of the nail, and various glue-like substances (resins).

Occasionally, a doctor may refer you to a foot care specialist who may try to file or cut the nail down the center in order to change the shape of the nail as it grows.

If any extra tissue has grown up around the inflamed area of skin, your doctor or foot care specialist may choose to remove the extra tissue to help it heal faster. He or she will numb the area before removal of any tissue.

Prevention of ingrown toenails

The best method of prevention is careful clipping of the toenails. Toenails should be clipped straight across – taking care to keep the end longer than the skin edge. This prevents the corners from digging into the skin. They should not be rounded or cut too short.

- Wear well-fitting shoes.
- Keep the feet clean and dry.

Fungus nails

Fungal infection of nails is common. The infection causes thickened and unsightly nails which sometimes become painful.

About 3 in 100 people in the UK will have a fungal nail infection at some stage of their lives. Toenails are more commonly affected than fingernails. It is more common in people over 55, and in younger people who share communal showers, such as swimmers or athletes.

What causes fungus nails?

- Spread from a fungal skin infection. For example, athlete's foot is a fungal skin infection of the toes. This may spread to the toenails if the skin infection is not treated early.

- Fingernail infection may occur after a toenail infection has become established. The fungus may spread to a finger if you scratch your itchy toes and toenail.

- Fingernail infections are also more likely to occur if you wash your hands frequently, or have them in water a lot. For example, if you are a cook or a cleaner. Constant washing may damage the protective skin at the base of the nail. This may allow fungi to enter.

- A nail that has recently been damaged is also more likely to become infected.

- You have an increased risk of developing a fungal nail infection if you have various other conditions. For example: diabetes, psoriasis, poor circulation, a poor immune system (for example, if you have AIDS or are undergoing chemotherapy), or in a general poor state of health.

- Nail infections are more common in people who live in hot or humid climates.

- Smoking also increases the risk of developing a nail infection.

- In some cases there is no apparent reason. Fungus germs (fungi) are common and an infection can occur out of the blue.

Symptoms of fungus nails

Often, the infection is just in one nail, but several may be affected. At first the infection is usually painless. The nail may look thickened and discoloured (often a greeny-yellow colour). Commonly, this is all that occurs and it often causes no other symptoms. However, it can look unsightly.

Sometimes the infection becomes worse. White or yellow patches may appear where the nail has come away from the skin under the nail (the nail bed). Sometimes the whole nail comes away. The nail may become soft and crumble. Bits of nail may fall off. The skin next to the nail may be inflamed or scaly. If left untreated, the infection may eventually destroy the nail and the nail bed, and may become painful. Walking may become uncomfortable if a toenail is affected.

Treatments for fungus nails

You may not need any treatment if your fungal nail infection is mild. However, if you do not treat the infection, there is a chance it will spread to other nails.

Serious fungal nail infections need to be treated. The main treatments are:

- Antifungal tablets.
- Antifungal nail paints.

Your pharmacist or GP will advise you whether you need treatment, and if so, which type you need.

During your treatment, you should start to see a new healthy nail begin to grow from the base of the nail bed. This is a sign that the treatment is working. The old infected nail should begin to grow out and can be clipped away over a few months.

Speak to your GP if you do not begin to see a new nail growing after taking your treatment for two to three weeks. Keep using the treatment until your GP says it is okay to stop. If you stop the treatment too early, the infection could return.

Preventing fungus nails

Studies suggest that in about 1 in 4 cases where the infection has been cleared from the nail, the infection returns within three years. One way to help prevent a further bout of nail infection is to treat athlete's foot as early as possible to stop the infection spreading to the nail. Athlete's foot is common and may recur from time to time. It is easy to treat with an antifungal cream which you can buy from pharmacies or get on prescription. The first sign of athlete's foot is itchy and scaling skin between the toes. See the section on athlete's foot in the next chapter for further details.

Also:

- Try to avoid injury to nails, which may increase the risk of developing a nail infection.

- Wear footwear such as flip-flops in public places, e.g. communal bathing/ shower places, changing rooms, etc.

- Consider replacing old footwear, as this could be contaminated with fungal spores.

Revolutionary breakthrough for fungal toenails

Leading aesthetic laser giant Cynosure UK are introducing the PinPointe™ FootLaser™, the world's first FDA cleared light-based device for the treatment of onychomycosis – better known as toenail fungus! A condition that affects 1 in every 100 people in the UK, and an estimated 10% of the population worldwide. Onychomycosis alters the look of nails, making them unsightly, and can be painful if the infection spreads, causing problems when walking, running or strutting in your heels! PinPointe™ FootLaser™ uses laser light to kill the fungus that lives in and under the nail without causing damage to the nail or the surrounding skin. Treatment typically takes 20 minutes with no downtime, side effects and only 2-3 sessions are needed! Alternatives include a course of oral drugs prescribed by a GP, or topical ointments, which are only 30%-50% effective, and often have painful side effects. In a 12-month study conducted on more than 250 patients, more than 70% experienced continuous improvement, and were fungus-free after a single treatment.

Hamish Dow, founder of the Dow Clinic in Newcastle says:

'The PinPointe™ laser offers a sophisticated, effective and technologically advanced treatment to kill the fungus that lives under toenails. With its unique delivery pulsing energy characteristic, this laser is a safe and comfortable side-effect free treatment. The alternative is a course of powerful tablets prescribed by a GP that must be taken daily, with results taking up to a year.'

Heel pain

Heel pain is a very common foot problem. The sufferer usually feels pain either under the heel (plantar fasciitis) or just behind it (Achilles tendonitis), where the Achilles tendon connects to the heel bone. Even though heel pain can be severe and sometimes disabling, it is rarely a health threat. Heel pain is typically mild and usually disappears on its own; however, in some cases the pain may persist and become chronic (long term).

The heel bone is the largest of the 26 bones in the human foot, which also has 33 joints and a network of more than 100 tendons, muscles and ligaments. Like all bones, it is subject to outside influences that can affect its integrity and its ability to keep us on our feet. Heel pain, sometimes disabling, can occur in the front, back or bottom of the heel.

Experts say that the stress placed on a foot when walking may be 1.25 times our body weight and 2.75 times when running. Consequently, the heel is vulnerable to damage, and, ultimately, pain.

Causes of heel pain

Heel pain is not usually caused by a single injury, such as a twist or fall, but rather the result of repetitive stress and pounding of the heel.

Plantar fasciitis

The most common cause of heel pain is plantar fasciitis, which accounts for four out of five cases. Plantar fasciitis is where the thick band of tissue that connects the heel bone with the rest of the foot (plantar fascia) becomes damaged and thickened.

There are thought to be two main ways that damage can occur:

- Sudden damage, such as damaging your heel when jogging, running or dancing – this usually affects younger, more physically active people.
- Gradual 'wear and tear' to tissues that make up the plantar fascia – this usually affects adults aged 40 years or over.

Wear and tear risk factors

Risk factors for damage caused by gradual wear and tear include:

- Being overweight or obese (very overweight with a body mass index of 30 or above).
- Having a job that requires you to spend long periods of time standing.
- Wearing flat-soled shoes, such as sandals or flip-flops.

Some less common causes of heel pain can also be diagnosed by your GP or a foot care specialist.

Symptoms of heel pain

Pain typically comes on gradually, with no injury to the affected area. It is frequently triggered by wearing a flat shoe, such as flip-flop sandals. Flat footwear may stretch the plantar fascia to such an extent that the area becomes swollen (inflamed). In most cases the pain is under the foot, towards the front of the heel.

Often the pain is worse on first rising in the morning and after rest; and is aggravated by prolonged weight bearing and thin-soled shoes.

After a bit of activity symptoms often improve a bit. However, they may worsen again towards the end of the day.

See your doctor as soon as possible if you experience:

- Severe pain accompanied by swelling near your heel.
- Numbness or tingling in the heel, as well as pain and fever.
- Pain in your heel as well as fever.
- Inability to walk normally.
- Inability to bend your foot downwards.
- Inability to stand with the backs of the feet raised (you cannot rise onto your toes),

You should also arrange to see a doctor if:

- The heel pain has persisted for more than one week.
- There is still heel pain when you are not standing or walking.

Treatments for heel pain

Your GP may be able to offer you medications and treatments for heel pain or may refer you to a foot care specialist for more advice and treatment.

Common treatments include:

- Rest – Avoiding exercise, running, walking and vigorous stretching.
- Avoid walking barefoot – Wear shoes with cushioned soles.
- Pain relief – You may find some relief by taking ibuprofen, or paracetamol.
- Ice – Icing the area will bring some relief.
- Steroid injection – Temporary pain relief, however not a solution to the problem.
- Ultrasound – A podiatrist will provide you with a course of ultrasound which has been very effective in relieving the symptoms.
- Insole/Orthotic therapy – A podiatrist will provide you with insoles or orthotics to support your foot.

Only relatively few cases of heel pain require more advanced treatments or surgery. If surgery is necessary, it may involve the release of the plantar fascia, removal of a spur, removal of a bursa, or removal of a neuroma or other soft tissue growth.

Preventing heel pain

A variety of steps can be taken to avoid heel pain and accompanying afflictions:

- Wear shoes that fit well – front, back and sides – and have shock-absorbent soles, rigid shanks and supportive heel counters.
- Wear the proper shoes for each activity.
- Do not wear shoes with excessive wear on heels or soles.
- Prepare properly before exercising. Warm-up and do stretching exercises before and after running.
- Pace yourself when you participate in athletic activities.
- Don't underestimate your body's need for rest and good nutrition.
- If obese, lose weight.

Plantar warts (verrucas)

Warts occur in a variety of shapes and sizes. A wart may appear as a bump with a rough surface, or it may be flat and smooth. Tiny blood vessels (capillaries) grow into the core of the wart to supply it with blood. In both common and plantar warts, these capillaries may appear as dark dots (seeds) in the wart's centre.

Plantar warts, also known as 'verrucas', can develop on any part of the foot. Sometimes dark specks are visible beneath the surface of the wart. When pressure from standing or walking pushes a plantar wart beneath the skin's surface, a layer of thick, tough skin similar to a callus develops over it. As the callus and wart get larger, walking can become painful, much like walking with a pebble in your shoe. Multiple plantar warts can form in a large, flat cluster known as a 'mosaic wart'.

What causes plantar warts?

Plantar warts are caused by an infection with the human papillomavirus (HPV) in the outer layer of skin on the sole of your feet.

There are more than 100 types of HPV, but only a few types are known to cause warts on your feet. Other types of HPV are more likely to cause warts on other areas of your skin or on mucous membranes.

Each person's immune system responds differently to HPV, so not everyone who comes into contact with the virus develops warts. Even people in the same family react to the virus differently.

The HPV strains that cause plantar warts aren't highly contagious. Therefore, it isn't easily transmitted by direct contact from one person to another. However, the virus does thrive in warm, moist environments – such as shower floors, changing rooms and public swimming areas. Consequently, you may contract the virus by walking barefoot around pools or gyms.

The virus also needs to have a point of entry into the skin. This can happen through:

- Cracks in dry skin.
- Cuts or scrapes.
- Wet, softened, fragile skin from prolonged water exposure (macerated skin).

Symptoms of plantar warts

Signs and symptoms of plantar warts include:

- Small, fleshy, grainy lesions or growths on the soles of your feet.
- Hard, thickened skin (callus) over a well-defined 'spot' on the skin, where a wart has grown inwards.
- Black pinpoints, which are commonly called 'wart seeds' but are actually small, clotted blood vessels.
- Lesions that interrupt the normal lines and ridges in the skin of your feet.
- Pain or tenderness when walking or standing.

Treatment for plantar warts

Contact your GP if:

- The lesions are painful or change in appearance or colour.

- The warts persist, multiply or recur, despite home treatment.

- The warts interfere with your activities.

- You have diabetes or nerve damage (neuropathy) in your feet – in which case, you should not use at-home treatments.

- You have a weakened immune system because of HIV/AIDS, immune-suppressing drugs or other immune system disorders.

- You have any doubt that the lesion is a wart.

In these cases, your doctor may prescribe a closely monitored treatment plan or consider a different diagnosis.

Plantar warts often don't require treatment. Most warts resolve on their own without treatment within a couple of years. However, if they are causing pain or spreading, they should be treated. It's much easier to treat a few small warts than several large warts.

Plantar warts can stubbornly resist treatment. Therefore, most treatments require patience, persistence and multiple interventions.

Key statistics and remedies for common foot problems

- The average person takes between 8,000 and 10,000 steps a day. The law of averages suggests that somewhere along the line wear and tear will give rise to ailments.

- The NHS spends £600 million a year on treating foot problems in people with diabetes, with a staggering £252 million of that spent on amputation.

- The UK foot skincare market is worth around £19m a year.

- Three-quarters of people get foot pain at some point in their lives and women are four times more likely to get foot problems than men, largely down to wearing high heels.

- Nonetheless, feet are far from immune from the problems countered by other parts of the body. Corns, bunions and blisters, all caused by pressure to different areas of the foot, are becoming increasingly common.

- Diabetes sufferers have an increased risk of infection in their feet because of poor circulation, which can cause healing to be delayed, and even minor cuts and sores can become infected. Diabetes UK recently warned that over a million people in the UK are unaware that they suffer from Type 2 diabetes, the potential pool of sufferers with related foot problems could increase notably.

- Athlete's foot, a type of fungal infection, is usually mild and responds quickly to treatment, although if left untreated can spread to the toenails and other parts of the body. It thrives in warm, moist areas of the body. A popular branded treatment is Canesten HC cream, which contains active ingredients clotrimazole and hydrocortisone. Clotrimazole, an antifungal medicine, is used to treat infections with fungi and yeasts, and hydrocortisone, a corticosteroid, is applied to the skin to relieve the symptoms of inflammation.

- Other marketable products for athlete's foot include Daktacort hydrocortisone cream, which is effective at treating inflamed athlete's foot and infections and inflammation between the folds of skin due to overgrowth of Candida fungi. Diflucan, a medicine used in certain types of fungal infections and which contains fluconazole, and Lamisil cream, incorporating the active ingredient terbinafine hydrochloride, an antifungal medicine, is used to combat infections caused by fungi. Athlete's foot sufferers bewildered by the array of options are confronted by other treatments on the market, such as Loceryl, Nizoral, Pevaryl and Sporanox.

- Corns, often suffered by women wearing badly fitting shoes or those who stand a lot during the day, are small circles of thick skin that normally develop on the tops and sides of toes. The two main types are hard corns, which are the most common, and soft corns. Hard corns are pea-sized and have a small, hard plug of skin in the centre.

84

The plug can press into the skin and cause pain and swelling. They often occur over a bony area such as the little toe. Soft corns are whitish and rubbery in texture and appear between the toes where the skin is moist from sweat or trapped moisture. They are extremely painful and can become infected by bacteria or fungi.

- Scholl Corn and Callus Removal Liquid has proven to be an effective panacea. It contains salicylic acid, which works by breaking down keratin, a protein which forms part of the skin structure, culminating in the shedding of skin cells from the affected area. It can also be applied to warts and verrucas, although patients should refrain from using the product for more than 12 weeks without consulting a doctor.

- Bunions, bony swellings at the base of big toes caused when the big toe bends towards the middle of the foot and the second toe, can be treated with bunion pads and painkillers. Lifestyle can, naturally, be preventative. Wearing comfortable, well-fitting shoes and avoiding high-heeled, pointed and tight shoes help, while flat shoes with enough room to move the toes is another shrewd choice. Padding over the bunion may also prevent further rubbing.

- Blisters appear when feet get hot and sweaty, making socks stick to the feet. The sock and foot rub against one another and the inside of the shoe, causing fluid to fill up between layers of skin.

  Once a blister forms it is advisable to cover it with an adhesive dressing or gauze and if the blister causes pain, cover the area with a soft dressing and change the dressing daily. If it becomes infected, a visit to the doctor for a prescription of antibiotics is called for. Nonetheless, Scholl Party Feet market a range of effective treatments, including blister plasters and gel plasters, sprays and pads, an ideal concoction that pharmacies stock.

- Another foot fiend is the verruca, a wart on the sole of the foot. A recent UK study of 1,000 children with warts found that 74% had common warts and 24% had verrucas. Boots Verruca Removal Gel, Salatac Gel and Scholl Seal and Heal Verruca Removal Gel are recommended treatments.

Chapter Nine

General Foot Problems

Very often, we overuse our feet but neglect to take good care of them. It is a known fact that the foot consists of a very complex structure of bones and joints, and more than 100 tendons, muscles and ligaments. These all work together to support the entire body, keep us upright and stable when standing up, walking, running, jumping and climbing. Imagine that each foot supports and endures the pressure of carrying our entire body wherever we may go.

Statistics show that millions of people suffer problems with their feet; one in five people suffer foot problems most days. This chapter is dedicated to describing general foot problems and complaints. There is a description of each foot problem, together with an explanation of the causes. There is also information within this chapter to assist you in diagnosing if you have a specific foot problem and the treatments available if you do. Being familiar with the signs of foot problems can help you get a head start on proper treatment.

Ankle sprain

Sprained ankles are the most frequent type of musculoskeletal injury seen by GPs and foot care professionals. Ankle sprains are common sports injuries but also happen during everyday activities. An unnatural twisting motion of the ankle joint can happen when the foot is placed on the ground awkwardly, when the ground is uneven, or when an unusual amount of force is applied to the joint.

Causes of ankle sprain

The most common cause of an ankle sprain is applying weight to the foot when it is in an inverted or everted position. Commonly, this happens while running or jumping on an uneven surface. The foot rolls in (inversion) or out (eversion) and the ligaments are stretched. Occasionally a loud 'snap' or 'pop' is heard at the time of the sprain. This is usually followed by pain and swelling of the ankle.

Symptoms of ankle sprain

The signs of an ankle sprain can include:

- Pain or tenderness.
- Swelling.
- Bruising.
- Coldness or numbness in the foot.
- Inability to walk or bear weight on the joint.
- Stiffness.

The severity of an ankle sprain depends on how badly the ligaments are stretched or torn. If the sprain is mild, there may not be much pain or swelling, and the ligaments may only be stretched. If the sprain is severe, one or more ligaments may be torn and the joint may be severely swollen. A severe sprain can also be extremely painful.

Treatment for ankle sprain

Your doctor will be able to tell if you have a sprain by asking you some questions about how the injury occurred and by examining your ankle. You doctor may also want to take an X-ray of your ankle to make sure that it's not fractured or broken.

Many doctors suggest using the RICE approach – Rest, Ice, Compression, Elevation – for treating ankle sprains.

RICE approach

Rest – You may need to rest your ankle, either completely or partly, depending on how serious your sprain is. Use crutches for as long as it hurts you to stand on your foot.

Ice – Using ice packs, ice slush baths or ice massages can decrease the swelling, pain, bruising and muscle spasms. Keep using ice for up to 3 days after the injury.

Compression – Wrapping your ankle may be the best way to avoid swelling and bruising. You'll probably need to keep your ankle wrapped for 1 or 2 days after the injury and perhaps for up to a week or more.

Elevation – Raising your ankle to or above the level of your heart will help prevent the swelling from getting worse and will help reduce bruising. Try to keep your ankle elevated for about 2 to 3 hours a day if possible.

Any ankle injury that does not respond to treatment in 1-2 weeks may be more serious. Always consult a doctor for a thorough evaluation and diagnosis if this is the case.

Preventing ankle sprain

The best way to prevent ankle sprains is to maintain good strength, muscle balance and flexibility:

- Warm-up prior to exercise.
- Wear appropriate supportive shoes.
- Pay attention to your body – slow down or stop when you feel pain or fatigue.
- Pay attention to walking, running or working surfaces.

Arch pain

Each foot has two arches. The longitudinal (long) arch runs the length of the foot, and the transverse (wide) arch runs the width.

Arch pain is the term used to describe symptoms that occur under the arch of the foot. When a patient has arch pain they usually have inflammation of the tissues within the midfoot. The arch of the foot is formed by a tight band of tissue that connects the heel bone to the toes.

This band of tissue is important in proper foot mechanics and transfer of weight from the heel to the toes. When the tissue of the arch of the foot becomes irritated and inflamed, even simple movements can be quite painful. This is known as arch pain.

What causes arch pain?

The arches are the primary structures of the body that absorb and return force to and from the body to the outside world when we are on our feet. When something happens to these structures, pain and injury may result.

There can be many causes of arch pain. Direct force trauma, ligament sprains, muscle strains, poor biomechanical alignment, stress fractures, overuse, or the tightness or lack of tightness of the joints in the foot may all cause pain in the arch.

Arch pain is usually felt as a stabbing sensation in the arch region. It can be felt in the distal (closest to the big toe) portion of the arch or slightly past the peak of the arch toward the heel.

Symptoms of arch pain

The most common cause of arch pain is plantar fasciitis. Plantar fasciitis is the name that describes inflammation of the fibrous band of tissue that connects the heel to the toes. Symptoms of plantar fasciitis include pain early in the morning and pain with long walks or prolonged standing.

Arch pain early in the morning is due to the plantar fascia becoming contracted and tight as you sleep through the night. When awakening and walking in the morning, the fascia is still tight and prone to irritation when stretched. When walking or standing for long periods, the plantar fascia becomes inflamed and painful.

Plantar fasciitis is caused by overstretching of the plantar fascia. Repeated strain can cause tiny tears in the ligament. These can lead to inflammation, irritation, pain and swelling. Arch pain is more likely to happen when:

* Your feet roll inward too much (over-pronation), see chapter 6.
* You walk, stand or run for long periods of time, especially on hard surfaces.
* You are overweight.
* You have tight Achilles tendons and/or calf muscles.

Four grades can be used to describe arch pain:

* Pain during activity only.
* Pain before and after activity, and not affecting performance.
* Pain before, during and after athletic activity affecting performance.
* Pain so severe that performance is impossible.

Treatments for arch pain

An accurate diagnosis from a health professional is important early in the management of arch pain.

If the symptoms are mild, management will generally just consist of advice about properly fitting footwear, stretching exercises for the calf muscles and arch and, if indicated, the use of foot orthotics.

If the symptoms are more severe, tape can be used to restrict motion and support the arch; anti-inflammatory medication can be used to give some relief. Orthotics are usually indicated.

If there is no initial response to treatment, further investigations may be necessary to check for conditions such as arthritis or a pinched nerve.

Self-management of arch pain

The initial treatment for arch pain, especially if it is of sudden onset, is the use of ice to reduce the swelling. Heat and anti-inflammatory gels can be a big help.

Activity should be modified – if you stand a lot at work, see if you can use seating more; if you run a lot, consider swimming or cycling for a while.

Use footwear that is supportive in the midfoot and heel area.

Preventing arch pain

You should seek professional advice on the adequacy of your footwear. Any stretching exercises that your healthcare professional may have advised you to do should be continued long after the symptoms are gone. Foot orthoses should be used if structural imbalances are present. Activity levels and types of activities (occupational and sporting) need to be adjusted accordingly.

Athlete's foot

Athlete's foot, medically known as 'tinea pedis', is a fungal infection of the skin of the feet. Despite its name, athlete's foot can affect anyone and is not restricted to those who play sports or participate in physical exercise. It is estimated that up to 70% of the population will have athlete's foot at some time in their lives.

Athlete's foot is a common name given to a fungal infection of the skin that predominately occurs in-between toes but can occur anywhere on the foot. If left untreated the condition can spread to other parts of the foot, hands and can even affect the face.

Athlete's foot can cause a great deal of discomfort and can affect an individual's quality of life. The skin involved may be red, swollen and may contain sticky fluid. Patients may also experience a scaly dry rash on the bottom and sides of feet. This type of athlete's foot is called a 'moccasin' pattern. Cracks or fissures can occur between the toes, sometimes accompanied by a soft white scale.

Many individuals with athlete's foot have no symptoms at all and do not even know they have an infection. Many may think they simply have dry skin on the soles of their feet. Common symptoms of athlete's foot typically include various degrees of itching and burning. The skin may frequently peel, and in particularly severe cases, there may be some cracking, pain and bleeding as well. Rarely, athlete's foot can blister. If athlete's foot is not treated the lesions can become infected and extremely painful.

What causes athlete's foot?

Many people have the fungus present on their skin but are unaffected by the microscopic organism. Conditions such as bruising or cracks in the skin allow entry for the fungus.

Fungi thrive on moist, warm environments, which is why this condition usually occurs in-between toes due to an accumulation of moisture.

It may also spread between individuals. A common port of entry is found in bathrooms, showers, swimming pools and changing rooms.

Not changing your socks on a regular basis can also encourage the build-up of fungi in-between the toes. Prevention is the key! Toe socks are ideal socks for people that suffer from athlete's foot as they are made from 90% high quality cotton and 10% elastane, for a perfect foot and toe fit.

People with excessively sweaty feet are more prone to this condition.

Treatments for athlete's foot

If you think you may have athlete's foot but are not sure which treatments to buy at your chemist or pharmacy, then make an appointment to see your GP first. Your GP may be able to diagnose accurately if you do have athlete's foot, and either refer you for specialist treatment if it is quite severe, or may prescribe athlete's foot treatments to combat the problem, for persistent infections oral antibiotic medication may be prescribed,

If you think you may have athlete's foot and would like to remedy the problem yourself, there are many over-the-counter treatments and products available to treat athlete's foot, however treatment is only permanently successful if the socks, shoes and the area affected are treated as well. It is important to continue treatment for the recommended time period even if the skin appears to have healed, since incomplete treatment frequently results in re-infection.

Be aware

Whether you develop athlete's foot or some other fungus infection, don't reach blindly for an over-the-counter treatment if you take any medications – ask the pharmacist about possible interactions and/or check with your doctor.

Preventing athlete's foot – your foot care guide

- Wash your feet often with soap and water, and be sure to dry them well after washing (especially the area between the toes).

- Do not wear other people's shoes or slippers.

- Choose shoes that allow air circulation (such as leather or canvas) rather than vinyl or other materials that do not allow the feet to 'breathe'.

- Wear sandals in warm weather.

- Always wear rubber sandals or waterproof shoes in public showers and locker rooms.

- Keep your socks dry, and change them if they become wet. Wearing cotton socks that wick moisture away from the feet is also helpful.

- Change shoes often.

- Antifungal foot powders can be applied to the feet or put in the shoes to absorb moisture.

- Avoid walking barefoot in any damp places. Sandals and water shoes can provide protection when using public pools and spas.

Blisters

Blisters are bubbles of fluid located under the outer layer of skin. The fluid can be clear, or it may be filled with blood or pus. This determines the type of blister the patient experiences as well as the cause of their occurrence. According to a survey conducted by Scholl, 30% of the population suffer from blisters.

What causes a blister?

A blister is actually the body's attempt to protect the underlying skin tissue from further damage resulting from various causes:

* Ill-fitting shoes.

* Friction (or severe bruising/pinching).

* Intense rubbing of skin against something.

* Injury to the skin due to heat, burns or sunburn.

* Moist skin is more susceptible to blister formation than dry skin.

* Allergies to insect bites.

* Viral/fungal skin infections.

Have I got a blister?

When the skin becomes irritated and a blister looks likely to occur, fluid collects underneath the outer layer of skin. The forming of blisters is painful, and size can vary; some of them are quite large and filled with a clear, watery fluid; if they're red, it means they're blood-filled and have resulted from severe pinching or bruising. If it looks like they're filled with pus, then the chances are they're infected. Infected blisters are painful; usually the skin around starts swelling and reddening and the patient may experience fever.

Treatments for blisters

Blisters do not require special medical attention. No special treatment is required other than keeping the blister clean and dry. Blisters normally dry out and heal within days. The skin provides a natural protection against infection, and all that needs to be done is to avoid further irritation. Medical assistance may be sought in case of a blister bursting, as this can lead to infections and further complications.

Here are a few tips for treating blisters and preventing infections:

- Apply a soft dressing (such as a plaster) onto the blister to prevent punctures; change the dressing daily.

- In the event of a puncture, press gently to remove the fluid and immediately apply an antiseptic (iodine) to prevent infections.

- As puncturing a blister can result in pain, applying an ice pack to the affected area may prevent or reduce pain.

- Keep the blister free from dirt or irritants by washing it frequently; after cleaning it, apply zinc cream to help dry up the blister quicker; however, avoid using zinc cream with a dressing.

- Avoid 'folk remedies' such as butter or vinegar.

- Avoid exposure to allergens or chemical irritants.

- If you've identified a potential start of blister, quickly apply a plaster, or any form of dressing, to prevent it from developing.

In the case of a blister, the most important thing to remember is preventing it from getting bigger and focus on minimising the chances of an infection occurring. Signs of an infection are pus and the occurrence of redness around the blister.

Small, unbroken blisters will eventually heal themselves. The fluid inside the blister will gradually be reabsorbed into your body. Once the fluid is reabsorbed, a dead layer of skin will be left. Do not peel it away! It serves as protection against infection until it falls off naturally.

Bunions

A bunion, medically known as hallux valgus, is a bony prominence that develops at the base of the big toe; this type of toe deformity occurs as a result of a change in position of the joints in the foot.

Researchers believe that flat feet or low arches reduce the stability in the joints of the foot causing the bone behind the big toe (the metatarsal) to drift away from the centre of the foot. The big toe, however, is prevented from moving in the same direction as the metatarsal by ligaments and muscles that pull it back. As the two bones move in different directions their joint protrudes, thus creating a bunion. The big toe is then angled excessively towards the second toe.

It is believed that bunions affect up to a third more women than men, and it may be caused by the wearing of tight, pointed or high-heel shoes.

Arthritis Care & Research published a study according to which one in three older adults have at least one bunion. The study also found that individuals suffering from bunions experience lower quality of life in social and physical functioning.

The chance of developing bunions increases with age. Bunions are believed to affect gait and balance, as well as increase the risk of falling in older people.

Bunions are thought to have a hereditary component, which means they tend to run in some families.

What causes bunions?

It is not known exactly what causes bunions, although there is evidence to suggest that family history and ill-fitting shoes are two major risk factors to developing bunions.

Shoes such as high heels may induce the formation of bunions. Due to the sloping foot bed and the narrow toe box, the foot is being pushed into the toe box causing the toes to be squeezed in together. Depending on factors like duration of wearing constraining footwear and skeletal maturity, the toes can adapt to the new position, leading to the long-term deformity. Other causes are:

- Poor foot mechanics, such as excessive pronation (rolling inwards of the foot) can lead to the formation of bunions.

- Conditions such as osteoarthritis or other neuromuscular diseases may lead to the formation of bunions.

- In some cases, trauma or injury to the feet may cause bunions, or if the ligaments in the feet are very weak.

- If one leg is longer than the other, the longer one is more likely to develop a bunion.

Symptoms of bunions

Bunions are often painful, although sometimes they do not cause any pain at all! However if you think you have bunions and are not sure what treatment may be required, contact your GP.

If you start developing bunions, you should notice:

- A bony prominence at the base of the big toe.

- A bursa (fluid-filled sac) develops where the bunion has rubbed against the tight footwear; this is usually accompanied by redness and swelling.

- Pain, this is due to the arthritic process in the joint as a result of bones changing positions.

- The big toe may press against, or overlap the second toe.

- The prominent joints may become sore due to rubbing against tight footwear.

- Pain and cramp in the toes made worse by tight-fitting shoes.

- Visible 'bumps' in the toe area of the shoes where the bony prominences have stretched the shoe material.

- Pain when walking or when wearing shoes.

As bunions form on the side of the foot and generally worsen over time, they can change the overall shape of your foot, which makes wearing shoes a painful experience. Bunions may be hereditary; look into family history for bunion cases.

Treatments for bunions

- Wear wide-fitting shoes; avoid high heels!

- If the bunion becomes painful, red or swollen, apply ice to the joint and keep the leg elevated on a chair or stool.

- Bunion night splints can reduce the size of bunions; this product will straighten the bunion while you sleep.

- A bunion shield can reduce the pain over the bunion.

- Performing stretches on your toes and feet will increase circulation, red blood cell activity and bone realignment.

- Orthoses are devices used to realign the bones in your foot; also they're an effective method to ease the pain caused by bunions.

In some cases, bunions can be treated surgically, although this measure will not completely remove the bunion. Surgery may be considered if the patient is suffering severe pain.

Preventing bunions

- Minimise the chances of developing bunions by wearing shoes that fit right.

- Your footwear should be wide enough for your toes not to be forced together and have enough room in the toe box so you can move your toes freely.

- Having a podiatrist examine your foot can help you purchase and use suitable footwear.

- Avoid high heels, and if you have already developed a bunion, make sure you protect it against further rubbing and worsening by taking appropriate measures such as bunion pads.

- Also highly recommended is to slip out of your shoes in the office or at work; despite any objections from co-workers, this will relax your feet and induce blood circulation.

Cold feet

Cold sensations to the feet can come from poor circulation and disorders of the nervous system as well as cold exposure and a low thyroid condition.

Having cold feet is normal. It's usually a response to low temperatures, but individuals may also experience cold feet in times of anxiety and nervousness.

What causes cold feet?

There are several reasons why your feet may feel cold. It may occur because of exposure to low temperatures, it could be a neurological cause (anxiety) or it could be the result of an underlying medical condition.

One of the major causes of cold feet is 'peripheral neuropathy', which can affect the feet and hands trying to protect core temperature, and that is sometimes seen in diabetes, chronic alcohol abuse or certain vitamin deficiencies.

Cold feet can also be a symptom of peripheral vascular disease, or PVD, which is a narrowing, or blockage of arteries due to a build-up of fat and cholesterol on the artery walls, a condition which limits the blood flow to the extremities.

Anxiety and nervousness also cause cold feet, because the extra activity from the nerves also causes arteries to constrict.

Body tissues could freeze due to extreme temperatures, and this state could injure the tissues. This condition is called frostbite, and it usually occurs on fingers and toes. When the skin is afflicted with frostbite the skin is frozen on the surface and the blood supply to that part is reduced; when that occurs on the feet, the result is the sensation of cold feet.

Your feet become numb and lose sensitivity to touch.

Symptoms of cold feet

The poor blood circulation that leads to the occurrence of cold feet may also be accompanied by a series of other symptoms.

The initial symptom is obviously the sensation of cold in your feet, as opposed to the rest of your body.

Over time though, your feet may start to tingle or feel numb and insensitive to pain and temperature, take on a red appearance and feel itchy. Your skin may develop a bluish or pale tint (cyanosis). In some cases, cold feet may be accompanied by sensations of heaviness and pain in the legs, buttocks, thighs, calves and feet when walking.

Other symptoms may include sharp pains or cramps in the calves, muscle weakness, poor hair and nail growth on the affected limb, slow healing wounds or sores, weak pulse in the affected foot, burning sensations and tenderness in your feet.

In more serious cases, when circulation is particularly poor, your feet may turn blue, and if you are suffering from frostnip or frostbite, they will appear white and waxy.

The unique characteristic of these symptoms is that they worsen during the night.

Treatment for cold feet

When the symptoms are mild, you may attempt treatment at home. For cold feet, a warm pair of socks and slippers should make the sensations go away.

Warm soaks are also very popular in treating cold feet. Soak your feet in a basin filled with warm water for fifteen to twenty minutes to relax your feet and induce blood circulation to the extremities. Do not soak your feet in very hot water! Your feet may be numb and therefore unable to register temperatures accurately and you could risk burning yourself! Also:

* Elevate your feet to remediate poor circulation.

* Avoid drinking alcoholic or caffeinated drinks! Instead, herbal teas such as green tea, ginger and chamomile will benefit your circulatory system.

* Aromatherapy also helps and provides a lot of relief.

* Massage your feet to promote circulation.

Sometimes cold feet signal an underlying medical condition such as diabetes, Raynaud's phenomenon or PVD.

Seek medical help when your cold feet begin to develop severe symptoms such as pain or discomfort, swollen or discoloured toes or a sore that will not heal.

Preventing cold feet

If you are prone to this condition, there are several simple steps you can follow in order to prevent it:

▨ Water on the skin allows freezing to occur 240 times faster than cold air; consider then waterproofing your running shoes with a water-repellent spray.

▨ Fleece-lined footwear made of leather or man-made insulating material is a very good choice.

▨ Choose footwear that covers the ankles, to keep snow and water out.

▨ Make sure footwear fits right; too tight and you constrict circulation! In the cold weather you may consider footwear half a size larger than normal to go with the thick winter socks.

▨ If you are on the ski slope, loosen your boot buckles in-between runs to allow more blood flow to the feet.

▨ Fit your shoes with warming inserts.

▨ Use socks made of man-made moisture-wicking fibres, such as acrylic or CoolMax. These fibres take moisture away from your skin and keep your feet dry which is essential for keeping them warm; socks must be loose enough so they don't restrict circulation.

▨ Improve your circulation through exercise and diet! Do aerobics several times a week to improve your overall heart and circulatory health

▨ Get sufficient magnesium, calcium and vitamins E and C. Food spiced with cayenne pepper, curry, ginger and cinnamon can increase your heart rate and get more blood flowing to your feet.

▨ Keep your cholesterol within acceptable levels.

- Quit smoking! Smoking increases the cholesterol levels in your blood vessels more than anything else, it hardens the artery walls and causes a constriction of the blood vessels; all of these individually cause a reduction in blood flow.
- Avoid a sedentary lifestyle and keep fit and active.

Corns

A corn is a painful area of hardened skin on the foot. They usually develop on the bony areas of the foot where high pressure is applied from walking/running and they're normally caused by ill-fitting shoes or the way your feet bear your body weight.

Corns (medically known as helomas) develop to protect your feet from the hardship they are exposed to daily.

Anyone who subjects their feet to any kind of pressure, are candidates for corn formation. More susceptible, though, are people with abnormal bone structure in their feet, or who suffer from different types of arthritis.

What causes corns?

The constant pressure on the foot that leads to the formation of corns is in most cases a result of poorly fitting footwear. Shoes that are too small, cramp your toes or have uneven soles are the most common cause for corn formation. The first signs are normally sore, tender areas on your toes which if ignored develop quickly into corns.

Being very active and doing a lot of exercise also puts pressure on your feet.

Bone malformations can cause discomfort when you walk. Individuals who suffer from bunions are more likely to develop corns as their feet press against the shoes.

Corns may result from poorly healed bone fractures, where the broken toe or bone has set out of place causing the foot to press oddly against the shoe.

Shoes, socks or stockings that fit too tightly around the toes normally cause friction in-between the toes and increase the chances of developing soft corns.

Think twice before deciding to wear a pair of shoes without socks. Skipping socks is an open invitation to corn formation.

Improper gait, such as walking on the sides of your feet, can result in corns developing on the pressured areas of your foot.

Individuals who have an abnormal bone structure in their feet or suffer from various types of arthritis are also prone to corn formation.

Symptoms of corns

The main symptoms for corns include the formation of a lump of hard skin over a bony area of your foot and pain when you walk.

In some cases corns can become quite painful and inconvenient and disturb a walking pattern.

They usually form on the weight-bearing portion of the sole, or in-between the toes as a result of chafing and friction. When they form in-between the toes, the patient is more likely to experience pain and great discomfort that will probably make them unable to walk.

A characteristic of corns is that they are regular in shape, and can be white, grey or yellow.

Also to remember is that corns tend to form more often on the outside of the first or the fifth toe, as they are the main points of pressure in the foot, either due to walking or simply exerted from rubbing against the sides of the shoe.

Treatments for corns

In normal conditions, corns do not require medical treatment. However, be aware of any potential underlying medical conditions that could have led to the formation of your corn in the first place. Consult your GP for advice if you believe there is an underlying medical condition causing your corns to form.

Seek your GP's advice for home treatment, he or she may recommend that you reduce the size of your corns by soaking your feet in warm water and then lightly remove dead skin using a pumice stone.

Depending on what is causing pressure, you may consider new footwear; use additional cushioning, alleviate pain by removing any pressure or friction on your feet.

Never attempt to cut the corns yourself, especially if you suffer from diabetes. You're likely to wound yourself, start bleeding and develop an infection!

In you suffer from diabetes, or any other medical conditions that cause circulatory problems, seek medical treatment.

Depending on your circumstances, a specialist may choose to trim your corns with a small knife, make recommendations in terms of footwear and padding, and prescribe orthotics. In some cases he or she may use collagen injections to correct extremely painful or chronically inflamed corns.

In some rare cases corns require surgery; however this is mainly for when the cause of your corns lies in a bone deformity (which may be a hammer toe or a bunion).

Preventing corns

- Wear well-fitted shoes; avoid shoes made of hard materials like leather, they constrict your toes and induce friction in-between them.

- Wear shoes with extra cushioning in the heel and ball for a balanced weight distribution on your feet.

- Avoid high heels and narrow-toed shoes! They predispose you to corns, foot pain and other problems because of the unnatural position of your feet.

- Dry well between your toes to avoid soft corns, and wear cotton socks. Chronic moisture damages your skin, so changing your socks often will help keep your feet clean and dry.

- Avoid tight socks that keep your toes from moving freely! When at home, it is highly recommended to avoid socks altogether and go barefoot!

- Soak your feet in warm water at the end of the day to soften your skin, and then file any rough skin patches you find to prevent corns from developing on areas that are already suffering from the pressure and rubbing.

- Lose any excessive weight to reduce pressure on your feet.

- Adjust your walking style; if you walk on the sides of your feet, the extra pressure will result in the formation of corns.

- Consume raw vegetables and natural juices to balance the level of acidity/ alkalinity in your system! An insufficiency of vitamin A, E or potassium in your system may encourage the formation of corns, so including fruit, vegetables and wholegrains in your diet may prevent the formation and recurrence of corns.

Flat feet

Most people's feet have a space on the inner side where the bottom of the foot is off the ground (the 'arch' of the foot). The height of this arch varies a lot from one person to another. Small children do not have an arch: it develops between the ages of 3 and 10. People who have a low arch, or no arch at all, are said to have flat feet. Sometimes they are said to have 'fallen arches', but as most of these people always had a low arch the term is misleading.

Causes of flat feet

In many people, it is just the shape the foot is. It may run in the family, and both feet are usually much the same and reasonably supple.

Rarely, the flat foot shape is due to something wrong with the way the foot formed in the womb; a joint may be malformed or two or more bones may be fused together. These feet are stiff and flat and the problem is usually obvious in childhood.

In other people, the foot tends to roll in too much on standing or walking. This may be due to lax ligaments in the heel (subtalar) joint or at the base of the big toe which allow more than the normal amount of rolling in of the foot. As rolling in of the foot is known as 'pronation' these people are said to have an 'over-pronated foot'. Due to the rolling in of the middle of the foot, the heel usually points outwards more than normal, as does the front of the foot. These people often have lax joints in other parts of their body too. This is the usual reason why children have no arch in their feet: children tend to have looser joints than adults. As they get older their joints tighten up and, in most children, an arch appears. It can be difficult to tell if a child has flat feet as the arches may not fully develop until the age of 10. The best way to tell if a person has mobile over-pronated feet is get them to stand on tiptoe, or to push the big toe up as far as it will go. If this causes the arch to appear, the foot is flexible and probably basically normal.

The people referred to in the previous paragraph have always had flat over-pronated feet. However, occasionally a flat foot develops later in life. This may be due to a ruptured tendon (the tibialis posterior tendon), or arthritis or an injury causing stiffness and distortion of the joints of the foot.

Some people with diseases of the nervous system or muscles such as cerebral palsy, spina bifida or muscular dystrophy may develop flat feet because some of their muscles are weak and their muscles do not work well together. Their feet are usually stiff and the deformity tends to get worse with time.

What trouble do flat feet cause?

Usually none! Some people with flat feet get aching in the arch, around the ankle or down the outer side of the foot, but all these can occur in people with 'normal' arches too. People with very over-pronated feet tend to wear shoes out very quickly.

Symptoms of flat feet

Most flat feet cause no trouble and do not need treatment. You may consider consulting your GP or chiropodist if:

▪ Your feet cause you a lot of pain that is not helped by wearing well-fitted shoes.

▪ Your shoes wear out very quickly.

▪ Your foot or feet seem to be getting flatter.

▪ Your feet seem very stiff.

▪ You cannot feel your feet normally or they seem weak.

Treatments for flat feet

In most cases, no treatment is needed as the flat feet cause no trouble. Most people whose flat feet ache feel better in well-fitted shoes: sometimes an extra-broad fitting helps. If you have troublesome, mobile, over-pronated feet, an insole, which prevents your feet rolling over so much, can help a lot. This would normally be provided by a chiropodist.

Children who have an abnormal foot because it has not developed properly may need an operation to straighten the foot or to separate fused bones. These are rare causes of flat foot in children: most children have mobile flat feet which need no treatment, or occasionally an insole because of pain or shoe wear.

People with flat feet due to a disorder of the nervous system may need special insoles, shoes or braces to support their feet or legs. A number of these people will need an operation to straighten their feet.

A flat foot due to a ruptured tendon or arthritis may be treated with painkillers and an insole in the first instance. Some of these people will need an operation to straighten their foot.

Foot odour

The medical condition of smelly feet is known as 'bromodosis' and the reason for it is that your feet have considerably more sweat glands compared with the other parts of your body. 33% of the nation suffers with foot odour problems

The main reason some people's feet smell worse than others is that some people sweat more than other people. This is just one of the many variable physiological qualities of human beings. This is also why sometimes your feet smell much worse than at other times – it all has to do with how much you sweat.

Foot odour is a kind of thick, often 'cheesy' body odour affecting the feet. In some cases, the smell can be similar to the smell of ammonia.

Smelly feet are generally caused by brevibacteria, which consume the feet's dead skin. Brevibacteria is especially active between the toes and on the soles of the feet. Brevibacteria is the same bacteria that cause some kinds of cheese to be pungent

What causes foot odour?

Foot odour is a common problem among males, but female smelly feet are also ordinary. Everyone who wears shoes or socks that do not allow the feet to breathe for a long time can develop foot odour.

The human feet have about 250,000 sweat glands. If they are fully covered for hours, they may perspire excessively. The moisture and sweat together create an ideal environment for brevibacteria and other fungi to grow.

People who engage in physical activities that cause the feet to sweat are especially prone to sweaty feet and therefore to smelly feet.

Certain kinds of socks can also make foot odour worse. Nylon, for example, does not allow the feet to breathe as much as cotton does. Nylon also does not absorb sweat as effectively. Female smelly feet may be caused by wearing nylon tights or stockings.

Symptoms of foot odour

Sweaty feet are not always smelly, but they are more prone to being so. The feet of a person with foot odour usually produces more sweat than a regular foot does. But because sweat is only water and salt, it does not smell on its own. It is when bacteria is attracted to the sweat that odour begins to emit.

Treatments and prevention of foot odour

Unless the smell is very severe, no professional help is necessary. Foot odour can be reduced and even eliminated by a few changes in foot care habits. Once the smell becomes serious and other symptoms such as itching and redness develops, though, patients are advised to seek the help of their GP or a podiatrist.

There are two ways to combat foot odour: one is to reduce bacteria on the feet, and the other is to reduce sweat that collects on the feet.

Washing the feet regularly with antibacterial soaps, wearing clean and well-ventilated socks, and allowing shoes to completely dry before wearing them again can all help decrease bacteria population.

To reduce sweating, patients are advised to only use shoes that let the feet breathe. Stay away from boots and other constrictive footwear. Cotton socks also help absorb sweat. Some even have moisture-wicking properties to keep the sweat away from the feet.

People with smelly feet should also invest in absorbent shoe inserts that 'eat away' odour. If the smell is persistent, doctors may prescribe strong anti-perspirant creams or powders, and sometimes even prescription drugs designed to combat bacteria and reduce sweat.

Hard skin

Hard skin is basically an area of skin that, due to certain factors, has become thicker, thus harder than usual. On the feet, hard skin develops where pressure and friction is applied regularly causing the body's self-defence system to respond. Nearly half (45%) of British people suffer from dry and hard skin on their feet which can be embarrassing and unsightly

Hard skin tends to develop more often on the ball of the foot, and it is often associated with various foot conditions such as flat feet, high arches or hammer toes. As a result, individuals who suffer from foot disorders may experience posture and walking alterations that put extra pressure on certain parts of the foot. As a result, the body forms extra layers of skin to protect itself.

Hard skin does not necessarily require treatment. Treatment should only be sought when it becomes uncomfortable and intrudes on your way of life.

Also, where hard skin develops on the area of the heel, be sure to treat it as it may lead to xerosis (cracked heel) which may become infectious and cause serious complication if you're diabetic or suffer from vascular problems.

What causes hard skin?

Hard skin is caused by friction and pressure on your feet. Our feet carry our whole body weight and are constantly pressed and compressed when we walk, run or even stand still. As a result, the body protects itself by forming extra layers of skin to 'cushion' our feet and absorb the everyday trauma.

The areas of foot more prone to hard skin are the heel, ball and sometimes the sides of the toes. Uneven weight distribution on the foot and improper footwear are very common causes for hard skin.

Excess pressure on the foot is also caused by certain foot disorders. High arches and flat feet are highly predisposed to hard skin. It also occurs over the bony pronations caused by hammer toes and bunions. Disorders of the metatarsal bone and slightly different leg length may alter the way you walk, thus creating pressure on other parts of the foot.

Bodily changes resulting from pregnancy, obesity and old age may also affect the distribution of weight on your feet and distort your walk. The added pressure and frequent rub will ultimately cause your foot skin to harden and possibly blister.

Walking around barefoot or running long distances also makes one susceptible to hard skin. Spending long hours standing up adds to the pressure on your feet, and so does footwear that is too tight and causes your foot to strain.

Symptoms of hard skin

Hard skin does not usually cause pain. The first sign of hard skin is the yellowish appearance of the skin, normally under the foot, that feels rubbery and tough to the touch.

The skin tends to thicken gradually under frequent pressure, and as the pressure goes on, the skin becomes harder to the point of callus formation. This could lead to a sense of discomfort when walking, and it usually goes away when you lie down.

Hard skin usually develops over the bony areas of the foot, so check your feet regularly for hard skin, particularly on heels to avoid heel fissures.

Treatments for hard skin

Hard skin does not have to be treated. It serves as protection against pressure and constant rubbing of the shoe, and it should only be removed when it starts to create discomfort and develops painful plaques or calluses.

For aesthetic reasons, however, a lot of people choose to remove the build-up of hard skin from their feet. For treatment at home, soaking your feet in warm water then rubbing them with sunflower oil should help treat the hard, thickened skin. To remove the piles of dead skin, a pumice stone may be used to gently scrub it off your feet. Remember to regularly moisturise your feet and keep the skin lively and healthy.

There are also medical alternatives to treating hard skin. Certain creams containing lactic acid should break down and soften the thick, hard skin. Always attempt home treatment first and only consult a podiatrist when these treatments fail or when your condition is caused by an underlying disease or you are diabetic.

In the long run, hard skin can lead to the development of corns and calluses which are more difficult to treat and may recur over time. When developed on your heels, it can lead to fissures and possible bleeding which is an invitation to infection.

Prevention of hard skin

Important to remember is that hard skin will keep recurring if the cause of friction and pressure is not removed or treated. Applying a moisturiser on your feet regularly will help keep your skin soft and healthy.

Prevent the formation of dry skin by carefully selecting your footwear. Avoid high heels and constrictive shoes that pressure the sides of your toes. Follow a special foot care regime and change your shoes often; wearing the same pair for too long will eventually wear down the heel area of the shoe and disrupt the balance of weight distribution on the foot.

Avoid using soap on your feet. The caustic soda in the soap will dry out your skin. Opt instead for a non-soap cleanser that will not rob your skin of its natural oils. Dry your feet well, particularly between your toes, then apply moisturising lotion to keep the skin supple and properly hydrated.

Soaking your feet in warm water then gently removing any dead skin cells will prevent the further development of hard, thick skin. Walking barefoot is again a very common cause for hard skin. Always protect your feet with cotton socks when walking. Where your occupation requires you to stand on your feet for long periods of time, take occasional sitting breaks and allow your feet to relax by temporarily eliminating pressure.

Treat any foot disorders to avoid the formation of hard skin. Bunions, hammer toes and high arches alter the way you walk which creates extra pressure on parts of the foot that become prone to hard skin. Keep your toenails trimmed and maintain healthy feet to avoid further complications.

Chapter Ten

Complex Foot Problems

Considering how much abuse your feet take every day, it may be worth your while to examine causes of foot pain or discomfort in a much more in-depth way, this can be done by consulting your GP or a foot healthcare expert. Often a simple fix is available to help you get back on your feet again. However, not all foot problems are easy to resolve with over-the-counter remedies and treatments.

Conditions such as hammer toes, arthritis and soft tissue problems such as trapped nerves (neuroma) and heel pain, can indicate that your foot problem may be a little more complex in nature and thus require a specific course of treatment and professional advice from a healthcare expert.

This chapter is dedicated to describing foot problems that may be more complex in nature than a common foot problem. There is a description of each foot problem together with an explanation of the causes. There is also information within this chapter to assist you in diagnosing if you have a more complex foot problem, and the treatments available if you do.

Arthritis

There are two main types of arthritis; these are known as osteoarthritis and rheumatoid arthritis.

* Osteoarthritis – Is the main form of arthritis and is known as the 'wear and tear' disorder. This type of arthritis can affect any joint. The big toe is especially susceptible due to the tremendous amounts of pressure placed upon it while we are walking. Osteoarthritis causes the cartilage to wear away and then causes the bone ends to fuse which results in stiffness and aching of the joints. Osteoarthritis can also follow a fracture or a bad sprain to the foot.

- Rheumatoid arthritis – Is a systemic disease, which affects the whole body. (A systemic disease is one that affects a number of organs and tissues, or affects the body as a whole). Rheumatoid arthritis affects all the joints and muscles in the foot. It affects more women than men and can be inherited. The insides of the joints become swollen and stiff. It affects the feet by causing a gradual collapse of the arch; the toes become contracted and draw back. Bunions are common amongst elderly rheumatoid arthritis patients.

The basics on arthritis

Arthritis comes in over 100 varieties. Osteoarthritis and rheumatoid arthritis are the most common. It affects several million people around the world.

We used to think it was just the elderly that were vulnerable to arthritis – not quite true. While it's more common in a mature age bracket, it can affect people of any age – even infants!

Arthritis symptoms

There is no single test that can check for osteoarthritis, so your GP will ask about your symptoms and examine you. He or she may also ask about your medical history. Your GP will look for bony outgrowths, swelling, creaking, instability and reduced movement of your joint, and ask if the joint is stiff for longer than half an hour in the morning.

You may have arthritis if you experience one or more of the following symptoms:

Rheumatoid arthritis

- Painful, swollen joints.

- Soles of the feet may feel tender. Patients often refer to this sensation as 'walking on pebbles'.

- Corns, calluses and ulcers may develop under the soles of the feet.

- The stiffness and inflammation is worse in the morning and after periods of inactivity.

Osteoarthritis

- Joints will be stiff and painful, and may be swollen.

- The pain may be worse after exercise.

- You may find you can't move the joint as much or as easily as before.

- Joints may make creaking sounds called 'crepitations'.

- As osteoarthritis progresses your joints may become misshapen and look knobbly. They may also be unstable.

You will probably notice that there are times when your symptoms are worse. There may be no particular cause, although they may be affected by changes in the weather or how active you are.

What causes osteoarthritis?

Despite many years of extensive research by medical experts and professionals; it is not known why the breakdown in the repair process that leads to osteoarthritis occurs. However, it is thought that several factors probably contribute to the development of osteoarthritis. These are outlined below.

- Joint injury or disease – Osteoarthritis can develop in a joint that has been damaged by an injury or operation. Overusing your joint when it has not had enough time to heal after an injury or operation can also contribute to osteoarthritis in later life.

  Sometimes, osteoarthritis can occur in joints that have been severely damaged by a previous or existing condition, such as rheumatoid arthritis

  Osteoarthritis that develops due to damage or another condition is known as secondary osteoarthritis. It is possible for secondary osteoarthritis to develop many years after the initial damage to your joint.

- Family history – In some cases, osteoarthritis may run in families. Genetic studies have not identified a single gene responsible for any of the areas affected, so it seems likely that many genes make small contributions. This means it is unlikely that a genetic test for osteoarthritis will become available in the near future.

- Being obese – Research into the causes of osteoarthritis has shown that being obese puts excess strain on your joints, particularly those that bear most of your weight, such as your knees and hips. As a result, osteoarthritis can often be worse in people who are obese.

What causes rheumatoid arthritis?

The cause of rheumatoid arthritis is not fully understood, although most research shows that it is an autoimmune disorder, meaning that the body's immune system is attacking one or more areas of the body. Some people have a genetic or inherited factor that makes them more likely to develop rheumatoid arthritis. Some medical professionals also state that environmental or biologic triggers, such as a viral infection or hormonal changes, can contribute to the cause of rheumatoid arthritis.

Treatment for arthritis

Your GP will carry out an examination to determine if your symptoms are concurrent with arthritis. There are several options to treat arthritis, your healthcare professional will discuss these with you.

Medicines can't cure osteoarthritis but they can relieve your symptoms. Pain may be relieved by over-the-counter painkillers such as paracetamol, ibuprofen or aspirin. Your GP will only prescribe stronger painkillers if your pain is severe. He or she may also suggest steroid injections given directly into the affected area.

You may wish to use non-steroidal anti-inflammatory drugs (NSAIDs) in the form of creams and gels that you rub into your affected joints.

Your GP can also prescribe creams and gels for arthritis.

If you have severe osteoarthritis, there are a number of different types of surgery that you may be able to have to improve the condition. Your GP will inform you on each of the surgical procedures used to treat arthritis.

There is good evidence to suggest that acupuncture is effective in relieving symptoms of osteoarthritis. Speak to your GP before trying complementary therapy or herbal remedies.

Preventing arthritis

* Wear appropriate footwear, which is deep enough to accommodate your feet.

* Have your foot complaints treated by a chiropodist regularly.

* Minimise and reduce strain – especially repetitive strain – on your muscles and joints. Things like repetitive actions, deep bending, lifting heavy weights, sports that cause abnormal wear, and so on. If your joints are aching or sore, there is something wrong and it should be checked out.

* Drink water. Your body is made up of 70% water. This includes that all-important cartilage between your joints. Keep up your water intake and your cartilage can do a better job protecting your joints.

* Protect your joints in colder weather.

* Exercise is good. And of course walking is good exercise too! You want to *use* your joints without *abusing* your joints. Regular exercise that overcomes a sedentary lifestyle is good. It doesn't have to be strenuous, just regular. A physiotherapist or occupational therapist can give you specific exercises if you need guidance.

* If a joint is swollen then the use of ice packs and anti-inflammatory creams can be of some benefit.

Burning feet

Medically known as Grierson-Gopalan syndrome, the burning feet syndrome is a medical condition that causes severe burning sensations of the feet.

The sensation of burning feet is triggered by a condition called 'neuropathy' (which is generally nerve damage in the legs). The damaged nerves send inappropriate pain signals to the brain, although there is no wound or injury.

There is a long list of medical conditions that cause burning feet, although diabetes is by far the most common cause of neuropathy in the legs.

Burning feet is a common complaint, especially in the elderly.

What causes burning feet syndrome?

Burning feet syndrome is normally caused by nerve or skin damage in the feet and surrounding tissues. Burns from extreme heat and chemicals or exposure to poisonous substances can damage the nerves in the skin causing burning feet.

There are physical as well as medical related causes for burning feet.

The physical causes include:

- Burns (including sunburn).

- Exposure to cold.

- Exposure to toxic or poisonous compounds.

- Foot trauma or injury.

- Nerve injury.

- Pressure on nerves.

Certain medications such as cancer chemotherapy drugs can also cause burning feet.

Certain diseases or medical conditions that cause burning feet:

- Diabetes (also the most common cause for burning feet).

- Alcoholic neuropathy (nerve damage associated with excessive alcohol consumption).

- Guillain-Barre syndrome (autoimmune nerve disorder).

- HIV infection and its treatment.

- Multiple sclerosis (diseases that affects brain and spinal cord functions, causing weaknesses, coordination and balance difficulties as well as other problems).

- Peripheral artery disease (narrowing or blockage of arteries due to a build-up of fat and cholesterol on the artery walls, which limits blood flow to the extremities).

- Rheumatoid arthritis (chronic autoimmune disease manifested through joint inflammation).
- Systemic lupus erythematosus (a disorder in which the body attacks its own healthy cells and tissues).
- Vitamin deficiency (especially vitamin B12 and folate).

In some cases, poor footwear can cause burning feet.

Symptoms of burning feet

A burning sensation may be the only symptom experience, or it may be accompanied by tingling and numbness. Depending on the cause, burning feet can be experienced while walking or even when resting. The duration of the burning sensation also varies; if caused by an injury, the burning feet sensation has as sudden onset; if caused by a medical condition, the burning feet syndrome develops slowly and worsens over time.

Amongst other symptoms accompanying burning feet, the most common would involve:

- Bleeding.
- Blistering.
- Numbness.
- Redness, warmth or swelling.
- Tingling, or other unusual sensations in the feet.

Burning feet may accompany symptoms related to other body systems, and these may include:

- Walking difficulties.
- Extreme sensitivity to touch.
- Foot problems, such as ulcers and bone and joint pain.
- Muscle weakness.
- Sharp pain than may be worse at night.

- Nerve pain.

- Tingling, numbness, or other unusual sensations in the legs.

Preventing burning feet

- Change shoes often; perspiration combined with friction and a lining material in the shoe that irritates your feet can be the cause of burning feet.

- Wear socks made of natural fibres, such as wool, cotton or silk; socks containing polyester don't breathe as well as natural fibres and retain foot perspiration, creating discomfort.

- Reduce alcohol consumption; alcohol dilates blood vessels, especially the capillaries, and contributes additional blood flow to the extremities causing extra warmth and burning in the feet.

- Avoid frostbite; this is a known cause for burning feet, so wearing suitable footwear in the cold reduces the chances for burning feet.

- Avoid long periods of standing or walking, and in case of tired or overworked feet, find well-fitting footwear with support, such as shock-absorbing insoles or cushioning.

- Light exercise and massage help to improve circulation in the feet.

Treatments for burning feet

As part of the treatment for burning feet, medical consultations must be carried out in order to establish what caused the condition to occur. A GP will be able to establish whether you have burning feet, and then allocate appropriate treatment, if the GP requires further investigation he/she may refer you to a podiatrist, rheumatologist or a neurologist who will be able to determine the cause for your condition. The specialist healthcare professional or doctor may take X-Rays, MRI and blood tests before prescribing a treatment. The treatment will most commonly involve magnetic therapy insoles, topical creams and general footwear recommendations.

Claw toe

A claw toe is a toe that is contracted to the middle and end joints. This can appear in any toe except the big toe, and it's caused by ligaments and tendons that have tightened, causing the toe's joints to curl downwards.

Often people blame the wearing of ill-fitting shoes, such as high heels or tight shoes, for the formation of claw toe. However, the claw toe deformity is often the result of nerve damage caused by diabetes or alcoholism that weaken the muscles in the foot.

The claw toe deformity causes your toes to virtually 'claw' and dig down into the soles of your shoes, creating painful calluses. Worse, because the metatarsal heads are forced to support the weight, open sores (foot ulcers) can develop on the soles of your feet.

Claw toe gets worse over time, and without treatment it may become a permanent deformity. The sooner the patient seeks treatment, the easier it will be to straighten claw toes.

What causes claw toe?

- Claw toe deformity is usually caused by a muscle imbalance in the feet.

- It can be congenital (from birth), or it may develop later in life as a result of other disorders.

- Claw toes can result from damaged nerves in the leg or from a spinal cord problem, however, in most cases it is difficult to establish a cause.

- People with flat feet (medically know as 'pes planus'), and people who have suffered traumatic foot injuries or have underlying diseases are more susceptible to developing claw toe.

- People who suffer from inflammatory illnesses, such as diabetes, rheumatoid arthritis or psoriasis are also at risk; cases of neuromuscular illnesses such as cerebral palsy are also more likely to result in the development of claw toes.

- Wearing shoes that are too tight or high-heeled, or shoes with a pointed toe box also increases the chances of forming claw toes.

■ Changes in foot anatomy may also result in the developing of claw toes; sometimes the metatarsal bones (the bones in the ball of the foot) can 'drop', creating a situation in which the toes do not make contact with the surface of the shoe. The toes may then contract at one or both of the joints to re-establish contact with the surface.

Claw toe symptoms

Signs of claw toe include visible deformity of the toe, pain and difficulty fitting into shoes.

The deformity caused by claw toe may include:

■ Your toes bend upwards (extension) from the joints at the ball of the foot.

■ Your toes bend upwards (flexion) at the middle joints toward the soles of the foot.

■ Sometimes your toes also bend downwards at the top joints, curling under the foot.

The affected toe may be painful or irritated, especially at the base or tip of the toe.

Your toenail may be malformed.

Areas of thickened skin (corns) may develop on top of the toe and calluses may form at the ball of your foot.

Treatments for claw toe

If you believe you have claw toe, your first port of call should be your GP. Treatment for claw toe depends on its cause, and if the toe joints are flexible or rigid. Although treating the underlying medical condition is crucial to your overall health, it will not reverse claw toe.

Depending on the level of flexibility in the toe joints, your doctor can make recommendations.

If the joints in the toe are still flexible, the doctor may recommend specific footwear, a splint or tape to hold your toes, cushion, linings and pads to help absorb force and place your toes in the right position.

If the toe joints in your foot are in a rigid or fixed angle, the doctor may recommend surgery in order to correct the condition.

Preventing claw toe

You may prevent claw toe by treating any underlying medical conditions that could cause it. You should:

- Avoid high-heeled or tight shoes, and wear shoes with a comfortable, roomy toe box.
- Stay away from loose or slip-on style shoes, as your toes will claw up in order to grip the shoe and hold it on!
- Try to wear shoes with a lace or a strap when you plan on being on your feet for long periods.
- Avoid straps or seams that may irritate your toe.
- Wear open-toed shoes in the warmer weather.
- Make sure that tights, stockings or socks are not too constrictive.
- A silicone toe prop will prevent the toe from deforming any further. Ask your GP about this.

Visit a podiatrist as soon as symptoms start occurring; claw toes are often a result of a functioning problem with your foot, such as a foot that excessively pronates (rolls in) or a structural problem such as pes cavus (high-arched foot). Your doctor will recommend you special toe devices to alleviate pressure and avoid the condition from worsening.

Foot gout

According to the UK Gout Society, gout affects around one in every 100 people. It's more common in men, particularly those aged 30 to 60, and in older people. It has been referred to as an acquired disease, or a form of arthritis. The inflammation and pain in the joint is caused due to a build-up of excess uric acid crystals. It usually affects the big toe but it can affect any of your joints, including those in your heels, insteps (arches of your feet), ankles, knees, fingers, wrists and elbows.

What causes foot gout?

You can develop gout if you have too much urate in your body. Urate (also called uric acid) is a chemical that everyone has in their blood. It's a waste product formed from substances called purines, which are found in every cell in your body and certain foods. Excess urate is usually passed through your kidneys and out of your body in your urine. However, the level of urate in your blood can rise if:

- Your kidneys don't pass urate quickly enough.
- Your body produces too much urate.

If the level of urate in your body is too high, it can form tiny crystals that collect in your tissues, particularly in and around your joints. This is what causes the swelling and pain. These crystals form at cooler temperatures, which is why gout is common in your fingers and toes.

Not everybody with high levels of urate gets gout and some people get gout but don't have high levels of urate. It's not known why some people develop gout and others don't. However, there are certain factors that can increase your likelihood of getting gout. You're more likely to have gout if you:

- Are a man aged 30 to 60.
- Are a woman who has been through the menopause, although women are much less likely to develop gout than men.
- Eat a diet that contains high levels of purines, which are commonly found in red meat and seafood – urate is formed in your body when the purines in foods you eat and old cells in your body are broken down.
- Drink too much alcohol.
- Take certain medicines, such as diuretics (water tablets), which increase the flow of urine from your body.

126

- Have a family history of gout.

- Have kidney disease meaning that your kidneys don't pass enough urate out in your urine.

- Are overweight.

- Have a medical condition such as psoriasis (itchy, dry and flaky skin) which can sometimes cause your body to produce too much urate.

- Have high blood pressure.

- Injure a joint.

- Are taking certain types of cancer medicines.

An attack of gout often occurs for no clear reason, but may be triggered by an illness, injury or drinking too much alcohol.

Symptoms of foot gout

You will usually have gout for a period of up to two weeks (an attack) and then it will go away, even without treatment. With treatment, this can be reduced to less than a week. You may only ever have one attack of gout in your lifetime, but for many people it returns.

If you have the following symptoms, see your GP:

- Severe pain in your joint.

- Swelling and warmth around your joint.

- Red and shiny skin around your joint.

- Mild fever.

- Firm, white lumps beneath your skin – these are urate crystals called tophi .

Your GP will ask about your symptoms and examine you. He or she will usually take a sample of your blood, which will be sent to a laboratory to measure the levels of urate.

Your GP may refer you to a rheumatologist (a doctor specialising in conditions that affect the joints) for further tests.

Your doctor may remove some fluid from your swollen joint with a needle. This usually causes no more discomfort than a blood test. If urate crystals can be seen in the fluid under a microscope, you have gout. If calcium crystals are seen, you have a similar condition called pseudogout. The crystals formed when you have pseudogout aren't urate crystals – they are made of a calcium salt called calcium pyrophosphate.

You may need to have an X-ray taken of your joint in order to rule out other conditions, but this is less common.

Treatments for foot gout

There are some medicines your doctor can prescribe to help ease the pain and swelling of an attack of gout.

Non-steroidal anti-inflammatory drugs (NSAIDs) may relieve pain and inflammation. If you have a heart condition, high blood pressure, kidney disease, lung disease or if you're over 65, these medicines may be harmful so you should talk to your doctor about taking them. If NSAIDs aren't suitable for you, your doctor may prescribe other medications.

Preventing foot gout

Identifying anything that brings on an attack of gout and avoiding doing these things is very important.

For example, you:

- Shouldn't eat foods that are very high in purines, such as liver, kidney and seafood (especially oily fish such as mackerel, sardines and anchovies), and certain vegetables (asparagus, cauliflower, lentils, mushrooms, oatmeal and spinach) – ask your doctor or a dietician for more advice.
- Shouldn't drink too much alcohol – especially beer, stout, port and fortified wines.
- Should eat a well-balanced diet and do regular physical activity to lose excess weight.
- Should drink enough water.

Ganglion cyst

Ganglion cysts are fluid-filled sacs. They can occur at any joint in your body, but are most common around the wrist. Ganglion cysts may also appear on the feet.

Ganglion cysts form when the natural lubricating fluid leaks out of a joint or tendon, making a little sac (or cyst).

What causes a ganglion cyst?

It's not usually known what causes the fluid to leak out of your joint or tendon, leading to the development of a ganglion cyst.

However, women are more likely to get ganglion cysts than men, and you are most likely to get them in your 20s to 40s. Sometimes, ganglion cysts form after an injury or after placing too much stress on a joint or tendon (for example, following repeated stress on the wrist in gymnasts). However, most people have not had an injury and the cause is unknown

What are the symptoms of a ganglion cyst?

The main symptom of a ganglion cyst is a swelling in the area affected. The cysts tend to be smooth and round and can vary in size. Some can be large and prominent, while others are so small that you can't feel or see them. Sometimes they shrink or grow, and may even disappear altogether, only to reappear at a later date.

If a ganglion cyst puts pressure on a nerve, you may experience discomfort or altered movement.

Treatments for ganglion cysts

Ganglion cysts are harmless and aren't cancerous. Many disappear on their own without any treatment, and often they don't cause any trouble. Because of this, most people don't need any specific treatment. Instead, your GP will just keep an eye on your cyst and wait to see if it disappears on its own over time.

- Non-surgical treatments – If your ganglion cyst is painful or is affecting how you move your hand (or foot), you can have it drained to reduce the swelling. This is called aspiration. A needle is used to puncture the cyst and the fluid is drained away. Aspiration is done under local anaesthesia, so the skin over the area will be numb but you will stay awake. Aspiration reduces the swelling, but it's likely that your ganglion cyst will come back later.

- Surgery – If you want to have your ganglion cyst removed and aspiration doesn't help, your GP may recommend surgery to remove it. However, there is still no guarantee that your ganglion cyst won't return and you may need to pay for the surgery.

Surgery to remove a ganglion cyst involves cutting the skin over where the cyst is, and removing it from the joint or tendon lining. Afterwards, the cut will be closed with stitches and covered with a dressing.

The area will feel sore, stiff and swollen for a few days after surgery. Complete recovery can take two to six weeks.

High arch

High arch is an arch that is raised more than normal. The arch, or instep, runs from the toes to the heel on the bottom of the foot. It is also called 'pes cavus'.

Cavus foot is a condition in which the foot has a very high arch. Because of this high arch, an excessive amount of weight is placed on the ball and heel of the foot when walking or standing. Small children do not have an arch; the arch begins to form between the ages of 3 and 10 and can occur in one or both feet.

Some people with pes cavus have clawed toes.

High arch is the opposite of flat feet.

Causes of high arch

Most cases of high arches are associated with nervous system disorders. The conditions that can cause high arches include:

- Cerebral palsy.

- Spina bifida.
- Muscular dystrophy.
- Polio.
- Stroke.
- Charcot-Marie-Tooth disease.
- Spinal cord tumour.

The cause of high arches cannot be determined in about one in five instances. These cases are called 'idiopathic', meaning the condition arises from an unknown or uncertain cause.

Symptoms of high arch

The symptoms vary depending on the severity of the condition.

Cavus foot can lead to a variety of signs and symptoms, such as:

- Shortened foot length.
- Difficulty fitting into shoes.
- Foot pain with walking, standing and running (not everyone has this symptom). With severe pes cavus, problems such as calf pain, knee pain and hip pain may be present.

Some people with cavus foot may also experience foot drop, a weakness of the muscles in the foot and ankle that results in dragging the foot when taking a step. Foot drop is usually a sign of an underlying neurologic condition.

Treatment for high arch

Treatments vary, depending on the severity of each individual person. A GP will assess your feet to determine whether you have high arches and may suggest a course of treatment for you or refer you to a foot care specialist.

In general, treatments include:

- Relieving pressure on different parts of the foot with silicone or felt pads.

- Removing corns and reducing calluses (best done by a podiatrist).
- Undergoing surgery on the soft tissues or bones to relieve pain.

Non-surgical treatment of cavus foot may include one or more of the following options:

- Orthotic devices – Custom orthotic devices that fit into the shoe can be beneficial because they provide stability and cushioning to the foot.
- Shoe modifications – High-topped shoes support the ankle, and shoes with heels a little wider on the bottom add stability.
- Bracing – A foot care specialist may recommend a brace to help keep the foot and ankle stable. Bracing is also useful in managing foot drop.

If non-surgical treatment fails to adequately relieve pain and improve stability, surgery may be needed to decrease pain, increase stability and compensate for weakness in the foot.

The surgeon will choose the best surgical procedure or combination of procedures based on the patient's individual case. In some cases where an underlying neurologic problem exists, surgery may be needed again in the future due to the progression of the disorder.

Prevention of high arch

People with highly arched feet should be checked for nerve and bone conditions. Identifying these other conditions may help prevent or reduce arch problems.

Hammer toe deformity

The hammer toe deformity is a common condition of the lesser toes, where the middle of the toes bends abnormally, causing foot pain.

Hammer toe deformities may be transmitted genetically where a certain bone structure abnormality in the toes is being passed on in the family. Footwear, however, is perhaps the major contributing factor to developing the condition.

What causes hammer toe deformity?

Hammer toes start to develop when the muscles get weak. In many cases, the weakening of the muscle results from diabetic nerve damage. This results in the shortening of the tendons that control toe movement causing the toes to curl under the feet.

Footwear is again a very common cause for hammer toe deformity. Tight shoes cause the toes to bend and the muscles to tighten. When bent for too long, the tendons contract and the muscles can't straighten the toe anymore.

There are other causes and risk factors associated with hammer toes:

- Genetics – Many individuals are born with a bone structure that predisposes them to hammer toes.

- Arthritis – This disrupts the balance in the foot and affects the motion and flexibility in the toe joints.

- Abnormal foot mechanics – Pes planus (flat feet) is very often a cause for hammer toe development.

- Injury – Such as breaking the toes or any other serious trauma may lead to hammer toes.

In many situations, not using your toe may ultimately lead to deformations. Staying in bed for too long due to prolonged hospitalisation or long-term immobilisation of the foot may lead to muscle contractures and consequently, coiled toes.

Symptoms of hammer toe deformity

One of the early signs of hammer toes is pain associated with shoe wearing; the shoe tends to irritate the affected toe, causing swelling, redness, blistering, inflammation of the bursa (bursitis) and the formation of corns. The toe will appear visibly bent downwards at the middle joint; the joint appears to 'rise up' causing the toe to contract in a claw or hammer-like shape. The joint becomes less flexible over time to the point where finding shoes that fit becomes difficult. Painful callouses may develop where the joint is bent, as well as on the ball of the foot due to the toe pressing down on the bone behind it. Hammer toes may develop along with bunions, and very often affect an individual's posture and balance.

Severe cases of hammer toes may lead to serious infections. Diabetics are highly predisposed to developing an infection where the shoe irritation of the toe causes open sores.

Treatments for hammer toe deformity

Consult your GP if you think you have hammer toe deformity, he or she will examine your feet and offer you a course of treatment or refer you to a foot care specialist for further treatment and advice.

Usually, non-surgical methods are efficient in treating the symptoms associated with hammer toe deformity as well as preventing complications and curing the condition.

Footwear change is usually the first treatment for hammer toes. Shoes must provide enough toe room to avoid rubbing and allow straightening. In the early stage of development, orthotic shoes allow toes to correct themselves over time. Shoe inserts and hammer toe pads will reposition the toe and relieve pain and pressure.

To help toes return to their normal position, a toe splint may be used; applying tape under the big toe then over the hammer toe and again under the next toe may help force the toe back into its normal position. The results should be the same as from using the splint. Remember to exercise the toes regularly; stretching exercises will help keep the toe joints flexible.

Non-prescription medication such as ibuprofen helps relieve pain. Consult a doctor beforehand to prevent complications.

Where pain and inflammation persists, your doctor may prescribe anti-inflammatory drugs and cortisone injections to relieve acute pain and reduce inflammation.

Where non-surgical treatments fail to correct the deformity, it usually requires surgery. This involves a small incision in the toe and releasing of the tendon around the contracted joint. The patient may walk straight after surgery in a post-operative shoe. Ice pack applications and elevation of the foot are recommended to reduce swelling and eliminate discomfort. Rarely, painkillers are prescribed.

Preventing hammer toe deformity

Firstly, it is important to point out that footwear is one of the most common risk factors for hammer toes, so carefully selecting your shoes will drastically decrease the risk of developing any foot conditions. Always look for shoes that are comfortable, adequately cushioned, low-heeled, with sufficient toe room and that allow your feet to breathe. Avoid pointed shoes, high heels, and vinyl and plastic materials (they don't take in air when your feet perspire).

Wear shoes that are about a half-inch longer than your longest toe. This way you maintain enough toe room even towards the end of the day when your feet start to swell. If the shoes hurt, don't wear them.

Exercise your toes regularly. If a hammer toe starts to occur, flatten your toes and stretch to keep the toe joint flexible. Curl your toes up and down repeatedly to enhance joint flexibility. Simple exercise will help restore flexibility in your toes.

Metatarsalgia

Metatarsalgia is a common foot problem described as pain in the forefoot (also known as the ball of the foot) associated with increased stress over the metatarsal head region, where the second, third and fourth toes meet the ball of the foot. Metatarsalgia is often referred to as a symptom, rather than as a specific disease. Common causes of metatarsalgia include poorly fitting footwear, being overweight, high-impact sports and medical conditions such as Morton's neuroma, gout and other forms of arthritis. The wearing away of the fat pad that protects the foot also gives rise to the likelihood of developing metatarsalgia amongst the elderly.

Causes of metatarsalgia

There are a number of different causes of metatarsalgia, including certain medical conditions (see below). Anything that adds extra strain or pressure on the ball of the foot can bring it on.

Common causes:

- Badly fitting footwear – Shoes with a narrow toe box or high heels can force the ball of the foot into a small amount of space, which puts more pressure on that area.

- Being overweight – This can increase the pressure upon the foot.

- Age – Older people are more susceptible to metatarsalgia as the fat pad that protects the foot can thin with age, making them more likely to feel pain in the ball of their foot.

- Bone structure of the foot – Narrow, high-arched feet or flat feet can increase the chance of metatarsalgia. Hammer toes (where the toes are bent at the middle joint) and a bunion (bony swelling at the base of the toe) can also bring it on.

- High-impact sports – Sports such as running or tennis put extra pressure on the foot.

- Stress fractures in the foot – These occasionally occur in athletes or walkers and cause pain to come on rapidly.

Medical conditions that can cause metatarsalgia:

- Arthritis, gout or inflammation (swelling) of the joints in the foot.

- Morton's neuroma – a common, painful condition affecting the base of the toes (usually the third and fourth toes).

- A build-up of fluid in the foot.

- Diabetes, which can cause the small nerves in the foot to become irritated.

Symptoms of metatarsalgia

Metatarsalgia causes pain in the ball of your foot that can be made worse by standing, walking or running. Some people describe the pain as feeling like they are walking on pebbles. Others describe more of a general aching pain. The pain can occur in one or both feet. In some people the pain is felt under one or two metatarsal heads; in others it is felt under all of them.

Metatarsalgia usually comes on gradually over some weeks rather than suddenly. The affected area of your foot may also feel tender when you (or your doctor) press on it.

Treatment of metatarsalgia

Your GP will examine your feet to assess if you have metatarsalgia and offer appropriate medication and treatment, or refer you to a foot care specialist for more advice and treatment options.

Simple measures can help to relieve the symptoms of metatarsalgia. These include:

- Resting with your feet elevated where possible.

- Losing weight if you are overweight.

- Wearing shoes that are well fitted, low-heeled and have a wide toe area.

- Metatarsal pads and orthotic inserts for your shoes may help to relieve pain in your foot by reducing the pressure placed on the heads of your metatarsal bones.

- Physiotherapy may also be helpful. This may include exercises to help a stiff ankle or exercises to help stretch your Achilles tendon if these are problems for you.

- Simple painkillers such as paracetamol and non-steroidal anti-inflammatory drugs may help to relieve pain.

Other treatment will depend on the underlying cause of your metatarsalgia. For example, if diabetes is the cause, you may need better control of the condition. If gout or arthritis is the cause, you may need treatment for these. Surgery is sometimes needed to treat metatarsalgia if other treatments have failed. This will depend on the underlying cause.

Prevention of metatarsalgia

There are certain things that may help to prevent some of the other causes. These include:

- Ensuring that shoes are well fitted, low-heeled and have a wide toe area. This may help to prevent some causes of metatarsalgia, including Morton's neuroma.

- Ensuring that you wear good, properly fitted footwear when running or doing sports with high impact on the feet.

- Losing weight if you are overweight.

- If you have diabetes, good control of your diabetes may reduce your chances of developing foot problems.

Morton's neuroma

Morton's neuroma is named after Dr Morton who first described this condition in 1876. It is sometimes called Morton's metatarsalgia or interdigital neuroma.

Put simply – Morton's neuroma is a swollen (inflamed) nerve in the ball of the foot, commonly between the base of the second and third toes. It is a common, painful condition.

What causes Morton's neuroma?

Morton's neuroma is thought to be caused by an injury to the nerve, but scientists are still not sure about the exact cause of the injury. The injury may be caused by damage to the metatarsal heads of the foot. All of these structures can cause compression and injury to the nerve, initially causing swelling and damage in the nerve. Over time, if the compression/injury continues, the nerve repairs itself with very fibrous tissue that leads to enlargement and thickening of the nerve.

Other causes of injury to the nerve may include simply having an incorrect walking style or an awkward foot structure.

These biomechanical (how the foot moves) factors may cause injury to the nerve with every step. If the nerve becomes irritated and enlarged, then it takes up more space and gets even more compressed and irritated. It becomes a vicious cycle.

Symptoms of Morton's neuroma

- Pain (sharp, stabbing, throbbing, shooting).
- Numbness.
- Tingling or 'pins and needles'.
- Burning.
- Cramping.
- A feeling that you are stepping on something or that something is in your shoe.

Initially, these symptoms may happen once in a while, but as the condition gets worse, the symptoms may happen all of the time. It usually feels better by taking off your shoe and massaging your foot

Treatments for Morton's neuroma

Your GP will examine your feet to assess and find out if you may have Morton's neuroma. It will help you to check things out in the early development stage. If you do have Morton's neuroma you may either be offered treatment by your GP or he or she may refer you a to a foot care specialist.

Treatment for Morton's neuroma depends on how long you have had the condition and its severity. Identifying the condition in its early stages will help to avoid the need for surgery.

Early treatment will aim to relieve or reduce pressure on the area around the affected toes. This may involve:

- A simple change in the style of shoes you normally wear. Wide-toed shoes that allow for width adjustment may be recommended.

- Padding to provide support for the arch of the foot, which removes pressure from the nerve.

- Anti-inflammatory painkillers and a course of steroid injections, which can help ease any pain and inflammation (swelling).

Pain can be relieved by resting the foot and massaging the affected toes. You can make an ice pack by freezing a small bottle of water and rolling it over the affected area.

In more severe cases, where early treatment options have not worked, surgery may be considered. This is normally done under local anaesthetic (the area is numbed).

Surgery usually involves removing the affected nerve, which often takes up to 30 minutes and can be performed on an outpatient basis (you go home the same day). There will be some numbness in the toes afterwards.

Alternative procedures are also emerging, such as releasing the affected nerve if it is trapped or removing the pressure on it. These other methods are being tried because in about a fifth of cases, a nerve stump can regrow when the nerve is removed and the symptoms may return.

Prevention of Morton's neuroma

- Avoid wearing narrow, pointed toe shoes.

- Avoid wearing high-heeled shoes.

- Wear comfortable footwear.

Sesamoiditis

Sesamoiditis is a common ailment that affects the forefoot, typically in young people who engage in physical activity like running or dancing. Its most common symptom is pain in the ball of the foot, especially on the medial or inner side. The term is a general description for any irritation of the sesamoid bones, which are tiny bones within the tendons that run to the big toe. Like the kneecap, the sesamoids function as a pulley, increasing the leverage of the tendons controlling the toe. Every time you push off against the toe the sesamoids are involved, and eventually they can become irritated, even fractured. Because the bones are actually within the tendons, sesamoiditis is really a kind of tendonitis – the tendons around the bones become inflamed as well.

What causes sesamoiditis?

Sesamoiditis typically can be distinguished from other forefoot conditions by its gradual onset. The pain usually begins as a mild ache and increases gradually as the aggravating activity is continued. It may build to an intense throbbing. In most cases there is little or no bruising or redness. One of the major causes of sesamoiditis is increased activity. If you have a bony foot, you simply may not have enough fat on your foot to protect your tender sesamoids. Also, if you have a high-arched foot, you will naturally run on the balls of your feet, adding even more pressure.

Symptoms of sesamoiditis

The most common symptom of sesamoiditis is pain in the ball of the foot and swelling. The pain often occurs on the medial or innerside.

The pain may be constant, may occur with, or be aggravated by movement of the big toe joint. The pain is often accompanied by swelling throughout the bottom of the forefoot.

Treatments for sesamoiditis

Treatment for sesamoiditis is almost always non-invasive. Minor cases call for a strict period of rest, along with the use of a modified shoe or a shoe pad to reduce pressure on the affected area. This may be accomplished by placing a metatarsal pad away from the joint so that it redistributes the pressure of weight bearing to other parts of the forefoot. In addition, the big toe may be bound with tape or athletic strapping to immobilise the joint as much as possible and allow for healing to occur. It is recommended to decrease or stop activity for a while. This will give your sesamoids time to heal. You should apply ice to the area for 10 to 15 minutes after exercise, or after any activity that aggravates the area. As with icing, anti-inflammatories will help the swelling go down so healing can begin. While the injury is healing, women should wear flat shoes on a daily basis. If home remedies do not work, see your doctor for a correct diagnosis.

Prevention of sesamoiditis

One of the best ways of preventing sesamoiditis, as with many foot conditions, is with the correct choice of footwear. Modern footwear such as trainers give the feet plenty of room to move, allow the bones to line up correctly, and have a wide toe box so as not to cramp the toes.

Tarsal tunnel syndrome

The tarsal tunnel is a narrow space that lies on the inside of the ankle next to the ankle bones.

Tarsal tunnel syndrome is a compression, or squeezing, on the posterior tibial nerve that produces symptoms anywhere along the path of the nerve running from the inside of the ankle into the foot.

Tarsal tunnel syndrome is similar to carpal tunnel syndrome, which occurs in the wrist. Both disorders arise from the compression of a nerve in a confined space.

What causes tarsal tunnel syndrome?

Tarsal tunnel syndrome is caused by anything that produces compression on the posterior tibial nerve, such as:

▓ A person with flat feet because the outward tilting of the heel that occurs with 'fallen' arches can produce strain and compression on the nerve.

▓ An enlarged or abnormal structure that occupies space within the tunnel can compress the nerve. Some examples include a varicose vein, ganglion cyst, swollen tendon and arthritic bone spur.

▓ An injury such as an ankle sprain may produce inflammation and swelling in or near the tunnel, resulting in compression of the nerve.

▓ Systemic diseases such as diabetes or arthritis can cause swelling, thus compressing the nerve.

Symptoms of tarsal tunnel syndrome

Patients with tarsal tunnel syndrome experience one or more of the following symptoms:

▓ Tingling, burning, or a sensation similar to an electrical shock.

▓ Numbness.

▓ Pain, including shooting pain.

Symptoms are typically felt on the inside of the ankle and/or on the bottom of the foot. In some people, a symptom may be isolated and occur in just one spot. In others, it may extend to the heel, arch, toes, and even the calf.

Sometimes the symptoms of the syndrome appear suddenly. Often they are brought on or aggravated by overuse of the foot, such as in prolonged standing, walking, exercising, or beginning a new exercise programme.

It is very important to seek early treatment if any of the symptoms of tarsal tunnel syndrome occur. If left untreated, the condition progresses and may result in permanent nerve damage. In addition, because the symptoms of tarsal tunnel syndrome can be confused with other conditions, proper evaluation is essential so that a correct diagnosis can be made and appropriate treatment initiated.

Treatments of tarsal tunnel syndrome

A GP or a foot care specialist will examine the foot to arrive at a diagnosis and determine if there is any loss of feeling. During this examination, the doctor or foot care specialist will position the foot and tap on the nerve to see if the symptoms can be reproduced. He or she will also press on the area to help determine if a small mass is present.

A variety of treatment options, often used in combination, are available to treat tarsal tunnel syndrome. These include:

- Rest – Staying off the foot prevents further injury and encourages healing.
- Ice – Apply an ice pack to the affected area, placing a thin towel between the ice and the skin. Use ice for 20 minutes and then wait at least 40 minutes before icing again.
- Oral medications – Non steroidal anti-inflammatory drugs (NSAIDs), such as ibuprofen, help reduce the pain and inflammation.
- Immobilisation – Restricting movement of the foot by wearing a cast is sometimes necessary to enable the nerve and surrounding tissue to heal.
- Physical therapy – Ultrasound therapy, exercises and other physical therapy modalities may be prescribed to reduce symptoms.

- Injection therapy – Injections of a local anaesthetic provide pain relief, and an injected corticosteroid may be useful in treating the inflammation.

- Orthotic devices – Custom shoe inserts may be prescribed to help maintain the arch and limit excessive motion that can cause compression of the nerve.

- Shoes – Supportive shoes may be recommended.

- Bracing – Patients with flat feet or those with severe symptoms and nerve damage may be fitted with a brace to reduce the amount of pressure on the foot.

Sometimes surgery is the best option for treating tarsal tunnel syndrome. A foot and ankle surgeon will determine if surgery is necessary and will select the appropriate procedure or procedures based on the cause of the condition.

Preventing tarsal tunnel syndrome

- Wear properly fitted shoes and orthotics, if necessary, to reduce the strain on the tarsal tunnel. Even if your feet are not flat, tying your shoes incorrectly or too tightly can stress the tarsal tunnel.

- Sometimes an enlarged or abnormal structure, such as a varicose vein, ganglion cyst, swollen tendon or arthritic bone spur, can take up space in the tarsal tunnel and compress the nerve. You need to address these conditions with your healthcare provider.

- Another cause of tarsal tunnel syndrome is an injury, such as an ankle sprain, that causes inflammation and swelling in or near the tarsal tunnel, which compresses the nerve. Treat injuries promptly and properly to prevent further problems.

- To prevent injuries that could lead to tarsal tunnel syndrome, warm-up properly before strenuous activities. Also, keep your foot and lower leg muscles flexible and strong with an appropriate flexibility and strengthening programme.

- Because overuse and repetitive stress can lead to tarsal tunnel syndrome, if you walk or stand a lot, rest your feet when possible to reduce the stress on the tarsal tunnel and tibial nerve.

- Other causes of tarsal tunnel syndrome include being overweight, which may cause excessive pressure on the tibial nerve; and diseases such as diabetes or arthritis that can cause swelling that compresses the nerve. Address any of these issues with your doctor

Chapter Eleven

Heel-Related Foot Problems

The heel is a padded cushion of fatty tissue around the heel bone (the calcaneus) that holds its shape despite the pressure of body weight and movement. It serves to protect the structures of the foot, including the calcaneus, muscles and ligaments. Heel pain and heel foot problems are very common foot complaints, this chapter explores some of the most common heel-associated foot problems.

Achilles tendonitis

The Achilles tendon is fibrous tissue that connects the heel to the muscles of the lower leg: the calf muscles. Leg muscles are the most powerful muscle group in the body and the Achilles tendon is the thickest and strongest tendon in the body. Contracting the calf muscles pulls the Achilles tendon, which pushes the foot downward. This contraction enables standing on the toes, walking, running and jumping. Each Achilles tendon is subject to a person's entire body weight with each step. Depending upon speed, stride, terrain and additional weight being carried or pushed, each Achilles tendon may be subject to up to 3-12 times a person's body weight during a sprint or push-off.

Achilles tendonitis is when the Achilles tendon becomes swollen, inflamed and painful at the heel.

An Achilles tendon also can partially tear or completely tear (rupture). A partial tear may cause mild or no symptoms. But a complete rupture causes pain and sudden loss of strength and movement.

Achilles tendonitis is likely to occur in men older than 30. And small tears in the tendon (tendonosis) are common among people older than 35 who continue activities that result in repeated stress on the Achilles tendon. These activities include sports, especially running.

> The Achilles tendon is named after Achilles: the ancient Greek hero of the Trojan War. Achilles was invulnerable except for one spot on his heel. After many adventures and victories he was killed by an arrow shot into his heel. As a result of the Achilles legend, the expression 'Achilles heel' came to mean a fatal vulnerability, and the tendon connecting the heel to the calf became known as the Achilles tendon.

What causes Achilles tendonitis?

Tendonitis due to overuse is most common in younger people. It can occur in walkers, runners or other athletes. Sports like basketball that involve jumping put a large amount of stress on the Achilles tendon. Repeated jumping can lead to Achilles tendonitis.

Achilles tendonitis may be more likely to occur:

- After a sudden increase in the amount or intensity of an activity.
- When the calf muscles are very tight (not stretched out).

Tendonitis from arthritis is more common in middle-aged and elderly people. A bone spur or growth may form in the back of the heel bone. This may irritate the Achilles tendon and cause pain and swelling.

Symptoms of Achilles tendonitis

If you experience the following symptoms you may have Achilles tendonitis:

- Pain in the heel and along the tendon when walking or running. The area may feel painful and stiff in the morning.
- The tendon may be painful to touch or move.

- The skin over the tendon may be swollen and warm.

- You may have trouble standing up on one toe.

If you are unsure as to whether you have Achilles tendonitis, consult your GP. Your doctor can tell if you have an Achilles tendon problem by asking questions about your past health and checking the back of your leg for pain and swelling. The doctor may ask: how much pain do you have? How did your injury happen? Have you had other injuries in the ankle area?

If your symptoms are severe or do not improve with treatment, your doctor may want you to get an X-ray and ultrasound scan, or an MRI.

Treatment for Achilles tendonitis

Once your GP has established whether you have Achilles tendonitis, he or she may suggest the following course of action or refer you to a foot care specialist.

Treatment for mild Achilles tendon problems includes rest, over-the-counter pain medicine and stretching exercises. You may need to wear well-cushioned shoes and change the way you play sports so that you reduce stress on the tendon. Early treatment works best and can prevent more injury.

Even in mild cases, it can take weeks to months of rest for the tendon to repair itself. It's important to be patient and not return too soon to sports and activities that stress the tendon.

Treatment for severe problems, such as a torn or ruptured tendon, may include surgery or a cast, splint, brace, walking boot, or other device that keeps the lower leg from moving. Exercise, either in physical therapy or in a rehab programme, can help the lower leg get strong and flexible again. The tendon will take anywhere from weeks to months to heal depending on the individual.

Although treatment for Achilles tendon problems takes time, it usually works. Most people can eventually return to sports and other activities.

Preventing Achilles tendonitis

- Wear the right shoes and sports shoes – The way a person walks, runs and jumps is related to their individual biomechanics: their bone, muscle and tendon structure. Achilles tendon injuries can be caused by common biomechanical issues such as high arches, low arches, having legs of slightly different lengths, etc. Biomechanical issues can often be addressed by wearing the right shoes.

- Warm-up before stretching or exercising – The term 'warm-up' should be taken literally: exercise muscles a little to heat them up just prior to stretching or exercise. Spend a minimum of ten minutes warming up. Warm-up examples include: walking slowly at the beginning of a long or fast walk, slow cross court movements and volleys prior to playing tennis; a brisk walk before jogging; jogging before running; lifting lighter weights before lifting weights, etc. Focus on the leg muscles, with particular attention to the calf muscles.

- Stretch between warming up and exercising and then again after exercising – Although there is some controversy about the value of stretching, many professionals believe that stretching helps prevent injury and that flexibility is a key component of fitness. Stretch the back, hip, thigh and calf muscles. Tightness in one can lead to undue strain and tightness on the others.

Cracked heels

Cracked heels are a very common foot problem that is also referred to as heel fissures. Nearly a third of the UK population suffers with cracked heels

Cracked heels are normally caused by dry skin and may develop complications when the skin around the rim of the heel is callused. When there is excessive pressure on the feet pads, your feet will tend to expand sideways; as the skin around the rims of your heels is dry (mostly due to a lack of attention to foot care), it cracks and the result is cracked heels.

Although for most people cracked heels are a nuisance and not a lot more than a cosmetic problem, when the fissures in the heel are deep, they may cause pain when standing up, and even bleeding which leads to infections.

What causes cracked heels?

Some people have naturally dry skin which predisposes them to cracked heels. The thick layer of skin (callus) around the rim of your heel, cracks when certain mechanical factors (such as the way you walk) increase pressure in the area.

Other causes include:

▓ Prolonged standing (at home or work, particularly on hard floors).

▓ Being overweight (this leads to excessive pressure on the fat pad under the heel causing it to expand sideways; this expansion will cause the skin around your heels to crack).

▓ Continuous exposure to water; standing too much in a damp area or under running water will rob your skin of its natural oils, leaving it dry and highly predisposed to developing fissures.

▓ Ill-fitting shoes, or an abnormal walking posture may have the same effect.

▓ Open-backed footwear, as it provides no support to keep the fat pad under the foot, causing your heels to expand sideways.

▓ Age is another major factor; dry, scaly skin loses elasticity with age leaving it prone to fissures.

▓ Deficiency of minerals, vitamins and zinc.

▓ Foot diseases and other skin disorders; if you suffer from Athlete's foot, psoriasis (a common and chronic skin disease), thyroid disease or diabetes, you are susceptible to cracked heels.

▓ Inactive sweat glands; without sweat your skin will be permanently dry and prone to fissuring.

▓ Flat feet and high-arched feet.

Cracked heels are also a result of poor foot care. So keep feet away from unhealthy conditions, keep your feet moisturised and maintain appropriate hygiene to avoid complications!

Symptoms of cracked heels

The first symptom of cracked heels is the development of dry, thick, hardened skin around the rim of your heel. This is called callus, and it's normally yellow or a discoloured brown colour with visible small cracks already over it. If they're not treated, as more pressure is being placed on the heel, these cracks become deeper, making walking or standing up difficult.

Visible patches of red, flaky skin or patches of peeling skin are also a sign of dry, cracked heels, and these require immediate attention to avoid dry skin infections. Some patients may experience itchy skin as well when the upper layers of dry skin shrink. This abnormal shrinking of the skin causes the skin below and around the heel to stretch resulting in discomfort and a great deal of itchiness.

Severely cracked heels are often thickly callused, with darker edges and deeper fissures that often resemble the cracks in dry ground. Where dark lines are visible in these cracks, it means dirt has accumulated inside the fissures.

Treatments for cracked heels

The best treatment for cracked heels is to prevent them from occurring in the first place, and you can achieve that by simply rubbing your heels with a moisturising cream regularly to keep your skin supple and hydrated. Special heel balms are available that contain descaling (keratolytic) or water-retaining (humectant) agents. Consult a doctor or ask your pharmacist for the best recommendation.

In order to eliminate the fissures in your heel, you will first have to treat the dry skin which caused them. Exfoliating your feet on a regular basis will help, although you will need to avoid harsh cosmetic scrubs and prepare instead a gentle natural scrub.

You may also treat dry skin and fissures by soaking your feet in warm water for 15 to 20 minutes at a time, and then using a pumice stone to gently scrub your heels to rub off dead skin cells. Be sure not to irritate small cracks; rinse off your feet, pat them dry, then apply foot cream, body butter or another moisturiser to treat them. Slip on a pair of socks and you'll feel better the very next morning.

To completely remove cracks, repeat this process as many times as necessary.

A few more tips to cure cracked heels, and some common sense rules, include keeping your feet clean, using correctly fitting footwear, moisturising regularly and drying heels properly. Remember to wear socks particularly in the winter, as the cold weather makes your skin dry, and ensure dirt doesn't get to your feet.

Consult a doctor if you suffer from an underlying disease (such as diabetes) and if you're overweight wear heel cups or heel pads to prevent your heels from expanding sideways.

Preventing cracked heels

- Ensure that your footwear covers the whole of your feet so no dirt enters the shoe.

- Wear socks, even in the summer, to help keep your feet moist.

- Drink lots of fluids to help keep the body moisturised from the inside out.

- Moisturise your feet daily and exfoliate using a pumice stone a few times a week to remove dead skin. Using a pumice stone in the shower or bath will help you eliminate calluses and prevent fissures.

- Apply a moisturiser while your feet are still damp as this will help lock in moisture preventing your skin from drying and cracking.

- Lose weight, if it's the case. Carrying excessive weight places too much pressure on the fat pad under your foot causing the skin on your heels to split.

- Keep your feet dirt free and exercise regularly, and if you've developed deep cracks, do not walk around barefoot (particularly on wooden or concrete surfaces) and seek treatment to avoid bleeding and possible infections.

- Wear 100% cotton socks and use sea salt scrub to get rid of dry skin.

- Avoid open-backed shoes as they cause your heels to expand encouraging the splitting and cracking of skin.

- Add insoles to your footwear and correct any walking abnormalities that you believe might induce cracked heels.

- Improve your diet if necessary. Dietary deficiencies may also cause cracked heels, particularly diets that fail to provide adequate zinc and essential omega-3 fatty acids. Zinc-rich foods include oysters, kidney beans, yoghurts and organic chicken. Omega-3 fatty acids are largely found in cold water fish and healthy oils (i.e. flaxseed). Get your vitamin E from green vegetables and wholegrain products and your necessary calcium from milk, organic cheese, yoghurt or broccoli. Organic meats such as beef, chicken and fish are rich in iron, and so are eggs and beans.

Include these in your diet and pay close attention to your foot care and decrease the risk of developing heel fissures.

Haglund's deformity

Haglund's deformity is a painful bony enlargement on the back of the heel. The cause lies in inherited foot structures that make individuals prone to developing the condition; however, an abnormal walking habit or unfit shoes may cause the condition to occur as well as worsen it once developed.

Haglund's deformity is also known as 'pump bump' due to being very common in women wearing high heels. High-heeled shoes make it difficult for the foot to stabilise itself which makes the Achilles tendon rub back and forth over the bony prominence even more, causing pain and discomfort. The rubbing first develops an irritation of the tendon. Repeated rubbing will slowly cause pain and eventually inflammation of the bursa (the fluid-filled sac between the tendon and skin). This swelling is called bursitis, and in may cause pain to the point of disability.

What causes Haglund's deformity?

Many individuals are born with particular foot structures that later in life induce the development of foot conditions. Haglund's deformity is primarily caused by inherited foot abnormalities such as:

- High-arched feet.

- A tight Achilles tendon.
- Walking (gait) patterns.
- Excessive running, walking or jumping.
- Foot muscle imbalance.
- Bone deformities inherited or resulting from foot injuries.
- Improper shoes.
- Trauma and overstretching are common risk factors for Haglund's deformity.

Obese people are very much at risk as the stress on their feet makes them susceptible to various foot problems. Athletes risk similar symptoms if they engage in long-distance marathons or extreme activities without proper conditioning and warm-up.

Symptoms of Haglund's deformity

Haglund's deformity appears on the back of the heel bone as a painful, red and inflamed enlargement or growth. It most commonly occurs where the Achilles tendon attaches to the heel bone. Footwear rubbing against the soft tissue near the Achilles tendon irritates the bursa while the back and forth movement of the tendon over the heel bone irritates the tendon. When bursitis develops the area becomes tender, warm and very sensitive to touch. It may impede shoe wearing and walking.

It's the inflammation of the bursa that causes the pain and swelling associated with Haglund's deformity.

Runners, young women in their 20s and 30s who persistently wear high heels and children from very young to the age of 15 who are very active, represent the groups that are more prone to developing Haglund's deformity because of their lifestyle and sporting activities.

Treatment for Haglund's deformity

Your GP will examine your feet and assess whether you have Haglund's deformity, and may suggest various treatment methods, in some cases your GP may refer you to a foot care specialist for further help and treatment.

A mild case of Haglund's deformity can be treated with ice compressions applied to the inflamed heel regularly. Apply a podiatrist-approved ice pack directly on the sore every hour for 20 minutes.

Oral administration of anti-inflammatory medications may help relieve pain and reduce swelling.

Anti-inflammatory creams and lotions are also recommended; unlike oral medications these don't pose any risk for stomach upset and other associated disorders.

Stretching exercises may relieve tension in the tendon, particularly for tight tendon legs that tend to compress the bursa and cause pain. Heel lifts placed inside the shoe may decrease pressure on the tendon and cushion the heel to avoid irritation when walking.

Physical therapy that includes foot massages, stretching and ultrasound treatment may reduce the swelling and treat the condition.

A podiatrist may prescribe you orthotic devices to control any motion abnormalities in the foot.

Preventing Haglund's deformity

■ Choose footwear that suits your foot type. Avoid high heels and hard-backed shoes that may rub against the back of your heel; open-backed footwear is highly recommended when the protrusion already exists.

■ Warm-up before engaging in sporting activities; avoid running uphill when training and run on soft surfaces (avoid concrete).

■ If the condition starts developing, wearing orthotics will help you correct any foot abnormality or walking habit that may increase the risk of bursitis.

- If you have a tight heel cord, stretching exercises will relieve tension in the Achilles tendon.

- When the bony growth on the back of your heel is large, you can either opt for open-backed and soft-backed shoes, or have your podiatrist remove it as prevention.

Heel fractures

Heel fractures (or calcaneus fractures) are potentially disabling injuries to the heel bone normally caused by high-energy collisions such as motor vehicle crashes or a fall from a significant height.

The severity of these collisions is caused by the associated complications that occur with a heel fracture; one in ten victims of accidents that cause heel fractures also suffers from spine ruptures and injuries of the hip and other parts of the skeleton.

There are more types of heel fractures, divided by the level of damage caused to the bone. In a stable fracture the broken ends of the bone align correctly for healing. An open fracture may cause serious complications. These fractures break through the skin and damage surrounding muscles, tendons and ligaments. When the bone ends are out of place, surgery will be required.

Bear in mind that surgery will not restore 100% of your bone function, and depending on the severity of the fracture, the rehabilitation period can last from 3 months up to 2 years.

Athletes, soldiers, construction workers, warehouse workers and overweight people are the most prone to heel ruptures.

What causes heel fractures?

Heel fractures are caused by high-energy shocks, and occasionally overuse. Athletes who return to sports after a long rest may shock their foot muscles and bones by attempting their usual performances without proper conditioning. Inappropriate equipment, shoes and an inadequate running surface may also lead to heel fractures. Certain bone diseases and foot conditions make individuals vulnerable to fractures. Osteoporosis (thinning of the bone tissue), certain bone development failures, hallux valgus and arthritis are high risk factors for heel fractures.

Strong physical collisions may also lead to fractures of the heel. You also risk fracturing your heel when landing badly on your feet or playing football or rugby (both sports involving a lot of physical contact and footwork).

Whichever the cause, the rule is – the greater the impact, the more bone damage it leads to.

Symptoms of heel fractures

Initial symptoms of heel fractures include pain and swelling of the heel and ankle. Patients with heel fractures experience progressive pain, bruising on the affected foot and instant inability to walk. In the case of an open injury, the skin around the fractured heel will be broken. Bone parts will appear coming out of the wound or haematoma (blood-filled swelling) and the patient will begin to lose strength in the foot and experience numbness (due to damaged nerves); however, most calcaneus fractures are closed which means the skin remains intact.

Treatments for heel fractures

Tell your GP exactly how you've injured yourself, and describe your symptoms accurately. Tell your GP if you're under any sort of treatment or if you're diabetic. Accurate information will enable your doctor to examine you correctly and diagnose your condition.

In the case of mild fractures where the fractured bone is not out of position, the doctor will recommend a cast to keep the bone ends aligned and secure healing. The doctor may opt for a walking cast, a splint, a cast boot or even compression dressings when the healing consists only in preventing further damage. Ice packs can be applied to the wound to reduce inflammation. Painkillers may be prescribed to relieve pain and antibiotics for infection and bacteria prevention. A tetanus injection may be required to prevent muscle spasms.

For displaced and open fractures, surgery will be required to restore the correct structure of the heel. The bone ends are reconnected and held in place with metal plates and multiple screws. This reduces the likelihood of arthritis and increases the potential for foot movement. The optimal time for surgery is when the swelling has disappeared. Keeping the foot immobilised and elevated will help reduce swelling. In the case of open fractures, the wound is exposed to the risk of infection. In this case, instant cleansing of the wound is required and immediate surgery performed.

For diabetics and individuals with poor blood circulation, non-operative treatment is recommended. They are usually prone to developing serious conditions following foot surgery.

Preventing heel fractures

Here is a short guide to preventing heel fractures:

- For athletes or anyone physically active, always warm-up prior any sporting activity; light stretches and other movements will reduce muscle stiffness and decrease the risk of injury.

- Beware of your existing foot conditions, choose shoes that suit your foot type.

- For active runners, change shoes every 6 months. It is important as the heel side of the shoes wears down with frequent use.

- Beware of rocky terrain! Choose an even surface for running.

- Beware of running uphill or running too fast downhill.

- Prevent recurrent injuries, protect your heel when engaging in any sporting activities; if you start experiencing pain, stop! And if you've injured yourself, allow yourself enough time for rehabilitation before resuming your activities.

- Avoid high heels, they lack padding and there is nothing to cushion the blow to your heels should you accidentally fall on your feet.

- Keep a healthy diet. Calcium and vitamin-rich foods help strengthen the bone.

■ Don't jump from any height! It's not easy to fracture your heel. It takes a lot of force to break the heel bone. A fall off a roof or a tall ladder is a common cause for heel trauma. Don't climb unless adequately equipped!

Heel spurs

A heel spur is a growth of bone that extends from the heel bone. The spur itself has no feeling. However the bony outgrowths usually extend from the heel bone into the soft tissue surrounding the bottom of the foot, causing inflammation of the plantar fascia (fasciitis) and pain throughout the heel of the foot.

Patients and doctors often confuse the terms 'heel spur' and 'plantar fasciitis'. While these two diagnoses are related, they are not the same. Plantar fasciitis refers to the inflammation of the plantar fascia – the tissue that forms the arch of the foot. A heel spur is a hook of bone that can form on the heel bone (calcaneus) and is associated with plantar fasciitis.

About 70% of patients with plantar fasciitis have a heel spur that can be seen on an X-ray. However, many patients without symptoms of pain can have a heel spur. The exact relationship between plantar fasciitis and heel spurs is not entirely understood.

What causes heel spurs?

The plantar fascia is a thick, ligamentous connective tissue that runs from the calcaneus (heel bone) to the ball of the foot. This strong and tight tissue helps maintain the arch of the foot. It is also one of the major transmitters of weight across the foot as you walk or run. That's why tremendous stress is placed on the plantar fascia.

When a patient has plantar fasciitis, the plantar fascia becomes inflamed and degenerative (worn out) – these abnormalities can make normal activities quite painful. Symptoms typically worsen early in the morning after sleep. At that time, the plantar fascia is tight so even simple movements stretch the contracted plantar fascia. As you begin to loosen the plantar fascia, the pain usually subsides, but often returns with prolonged standing or walking.

Heel spurs form in some patients who have plantar fasciitis, and tend to occur in patients who have had the problem for a prolonged period of time. While about 70% of patients with plantar fasciitis have a heel spur, X-rays also show about 50% of patients with no symptoms of plantar fasciitis also have a heel spur.

The calcaneal spur is seen most often in persons over the age of 40. The condition can also be associated with osteoarthritis, rheumatoid arthritis, poor circulation of the blood and other degenerative diseases. Men and women are equally likely to have them.

Symptoms of heel spurs

Although it may take years to become a problem, once it appears, it may cause considerable suffering. Because of proximity to the tendons, the spur is a source of continuous painful aching. The sensation has been described as 'a toothache in the foot'. When you place your weight on the heel, the pain can be sufficient enough to immobilise you.

The pain caused by a calcaneal spur is not the result of the pressure of weight on the point of the spur, but results from inflammation around the tendons where they attach to the heel bone. You might expect the pain to increase as you walk on the spur, but actually it decreases. The pain is most severe when you start to walk after a rest. The nerves and capillaries adapt themselves to the situation as you walk. When you rest, the nerves and capillaries rest also. Then, as you begin to move about again, extreme demands are made on the blood vessels and nerves, which will cause pain until they again adjust to the spur.

If excessive strain has been placed on the foot the day before, the pain may also be greater. A sudden strain, as might be produced by leaping or jumping, can also increase the pain. The pain might be localised at first, but continued walking and standing will soon cause the entire heel to become tender and painful.

Treatment for heel spurs

Your GP will examine your feet and assess whether you have heel spurs, you may be offered treatment and medication by your GP or he or she will refer you for further foot care treatment from a specialist.

Bone spurs rarely require treatment unless they are causing frequent pain or damaging other tissues. Because heel spurs and plantar fasciitis are so closely related, they are usually treated the same way.

Treatment involves rest, especially from the activity that is contributing to the condition and making symptoms worse (although this may not be easy to discover, as problems can manifest several hours or days after the harmful activity has occurred).

If you experience pain your GP will offer you pain relief for the symptoms.

Proper footwear is imperative.

Plantar fasciitis

The plantar fascia is a band of tissue, much like a tendon, that starts at your heel and goes along the bottom of your foot. It attaches to each one of the bones that form the ball of your foot. The plantar fascia works like a rubber band between the heel and the ball of your foot to form the arch of your foot. If the band is short, you'll have a high arch, and if it's long, you'll have a low arch, what some people call flat feet. A pad of fat in your heel covers the plantar fascia to help absorb the shock of walking. Damage to the plantar fascia can be a cause of heel pain.

What causes plantar fasciitis?

As a person gets older, the plantar fascia becomes less like a rubber band and more like a rope that doesn't stretch very well. The fat pad on the heel becomes thinner and can't absorb as much of the shock caused by walking. The extra shock damages the plantar fascia and may cause it to swell, tear or bruise. You may notice a bruise or swelling on your heel.

Other risk factors for plantar fasciitis include:

- Being overweight or obese.
- Diabetes.
- Spending most of the day on your feet.
- Becoming very active in a short period of time.
- Being flat-footed or having a high arch.

Symptoms of plantar fasciitis

If you have pain in your heel when you stand up for the first time in the morning, you may have plantar fasciitis. Most people with plantar fasciitis say the pain is like a knife or a pin sticking into the bottom of the foot. After you've been standing for a while, the pain becomes more like a dull ache. If you sit down for any length of time, the sharp pain will come back when you stand up again.

Treatments for plantar fasciitis

You GP will examine your feet and assess whether you have plantar fasciitis, if you do he or she may refer you to a foot care specialist for more advice and treatment. Your GP may also give you medication and advice, such as:

- If you walk or run a lot, you may be asked to cut back a little. You probably won't need to stop walking or running altogether.
- If you have either flat feet or a high arch, your doctor or foot care specialist may recommend inserts for your shoes called orthotics. Orthotics are arch supports. You will need to be fitted for them.
- If you are overweight, weight loss will be recommended.
- If your job involves standing on a hard floor or standing in one spot for long periods, you may be advised to place some type of padding on the floor where you stand.

Prevention for plantar fasciitis

- Take care of your feet. Wear shoes with good arch support and heel cushioning. If your work requires you to stand on hard surfaces, stand on a thick rubber mat to reduce stress on your feet.

- Do exercises to stretch the Achilles tendon at the back of the heel. This is especially important before sports, but it is helpful for non-athletic people as well. Ask your doctor about recommendations for a stretching routine.

- Stay at a healthy weight for your height.

- Establish good exercise habits. Increase your exercise levels gradually, and wear supportive shoes.

- If you run, alternate running with other sports that will not cause heel pain.

- Put on supportive shoes as soon as you get out of bed. Going barefoot or wearing slippers puts stress on your feet.

Chapter Twelve

Diabetes and Foot Problems

Diabetes is a serious disease that can develop from lack of insulin production in the body or due to the inability of the body's insulin to perform its normal everyday functions. Insulin is a substance produced by the pancreas gland that helps process the food we eat and turn it into energy. Diabetes affects hundreds of thousands of people in the UK.

Diabetes is classified into 2 different types: Type 1 and Type 2. Type 1 is usually associated with juvenile diabetes and is often linked to heredity. Type 2, commonly referred to as adult onset diabetes, is characterised by elevated blood sugars, often in people who are overweight or have not attended to their diet properly. Many complications can be associated with diabetes. Diabetes disrupts the vascular system, affecting many areas of the body such as the eyes, kidneys, legs and feet. People with diabetes should pay special attention to their feet.

Neuropathy

There are three types of neuropathy, and they can all affect your feet:

■ Sensory neuropathy – This affects the nerves that carry messages from the skin, bones and muscles to the brain and affects how we feel temperature, pain and other sensations. It is the most common form of neuropathy, mainly occurring in nerves in the feet and legs, and can lead to a loss of feeling and a failure to sense pain. This could mean that you might develop a blister or minor burn without realising it, which, if not treated properly, could become infected or develop into an ulcer.

- Motor neuropathy – This affects the nerves responsible for sending messages to the muscles about movements, such as walking. If the nerves supplying your feet are affected it could cause your feet to alter shape. Your toes may become clawed (curled) as your arch/instep becomes more pronounced or the arch may 'fall' causing flat feet. This can cause the bones in your foot to fracture (break) when stressed.

- Autonomic neuropathy – This affects the nerves which control activities which our bodies carry out all the time, which we have no control over. Damage to these nerves may affect your sweat glands, reducing secretions and making your skin dry and inelastic. If not looked after, the skin may crack and become sore and prone to infection.

Diabetes may also affect the circulation by causing the arteries to become 'furred up' (artherosclerosis). This can affect all the major blood vessels, especially those supplying the feet. Without a good blood supply, you will have problems with cuts and sores which do not heal very well, and as a result of poor circulation you may also suffer from cramp and pain in your legs and/or feet. If your diabetes is poorly controlled, you run greater risk of poor circulation and the problems associated with a poor blood supply to your feet. High blood pressure, a high fat content in your diet and, in particular, smoking, all increase the risk of poor circulation.

Treatment and prevention

If you are a diabetic, you should be particularly alert to any problems you may be having with your feet. It is very important for diabetics with neuropathy to take necessary precautions to prevent injury and keep their feet healthy. If you have diabetes and are experiencing a foot problem, immediately consult your foot doctor.

Foot care and diabetes

Proper foot care is especially critical for diabetics because they are prone to foot problems such as:

- Loss of feeling in their feet.

- Changes in the shape of their feet.

- Foot ulcers or sores that do not heal.

Simple daily foot care can prevent serious problems. According to the National Institute of Health (NIH), the following simple everyday steps will help prevent serious complications from diabetes:

- Take care of your diabetes – Make healthy lifestyle choices to keep your blood sugar close to normal. Work with your healthcare team to create a diabetes plan that fits your lifestyle characteristics.

- Check your feet every day – You may have foot problems that you may not be aware of. Check your feet for cuts, sores, red spots, swelling or infected toenails. Checking your feet should become part of your daily routine. If you have trouble bending over to see your feet, use a plastic mirror to help. You can also ask a family member to help you. Be sure to call your doctor immediately if a cut, sore, blister or bruise on your foot does not heal after one day.

- Wash your feet every day – Wash your feet in warm not hot water. Do not soak your feet because your skin will get dry. Before bathing or showering, test the water to make sure it is not too hot. You should use a thermometer or your elbow. Dry your feet well. Be sure to dry between your toes. Use talcum powder to keep the skin dry between the toes.

- Keep the skin soft and smooth – Rub a thin coat of skin lotion or cream on the tops and bottoms of the feet. Do not put lotion between your toes, because this might cause infection.

- Wear shoes and socks at all times – Do not walk barefoot, not even indoors. It is extremely easy to step on something and hurt your feet. Always wear seamless socks, stockings and nylons with your shoes to help avoid the possibility of blisters and sores developing. Be sure to choose seamless socks that are made of materials that wick moisture away from your feet and absorb shock. Socks made of these materials help keep your feet dry. Always check the insides of your shoes before putting them on. Make sure the lining is smooth and there are no foreign objects in the shoe, such as pebbles. Wear shoes that fit well and protect your feet.

- Protect your feet from hot and cold – Always wear shoes at the beach or on hot pavements. Put sunscreen on the tops of your feet for protection from the sun. Keep your feet away from radiators or open fires. Do not use hot water bottles or heating pads on your feet. If your feet are cold, wear seamless socks at night. Lined boots are good to keep your feet warm in the winter. Choose padded socks to protect your feet and make walking more comfortable. In cold weather, check your feet often to keep your feet warm to avoid frostbite.

- Keep the blood flowing to your feet – Put your feet up when you are sitting. Wiggle your toes for 5 minutes, two or three times a day. Move your ankles up and down and in and out to improve blood flow in your feet and legs. Do not cross your legs for long periods of time. Do not wear tight socks, elastic or rubber bands or garters around your legs. Do not wear restrictive footwear or foot products. Foot products that can cut off circulation to the feet, such as products with elastic, should not be worn by diabetics. Do not smoke. Smoking reduces blood flow to your feet. If you have high blood pressure or high cholesterol, work with your healthcare team to lower it.

- Be more active – Ask your doctor to plan an exercise programme that is right for you. Walking, dancing, swimming and cycling are good forms of exercise that are easy on the feet. Avoid all activities that are hard on the feet, such as running and jumping. Always include a short warm-up or cool-down period. Wear protective walking or athletic shoes that fit well and offer good support.

- Communicate with your doctor – Ask your doctor to check the sense of feeling and pulses in your feet at least once a year. Ask your doctor to tell you immediately if you have serious foot problems. Ask your doctor for proper foot care tips and for the name of your local podiatrist.

Diabetic foot

A diabetic foot is a foot that develops pathological symptoms resulting from diabetes.

Diabetes patients must pay extra attention to their foot care. Any wounding, heel fissures, blisters or untreated corns can lead to infections and, in worse cases, foot ulcerations and possible amputations. Not everyone who suffers from diabetes develops foot problems. If the patient keeps their condition well under control, the chances of developing foot problems decrease.

However, as complete control of diabetes is not always possible, small cuts or injuries to the foot may result in infections which may lead to neuropathy (damaged nerves) and peripheral vascular disease (blocked arteries) in the legs; these conditions are hardly ever reversible and may result in amputation. As neuropathy results in loss of feeling in the feet, diabetic nerve damage means the patient may not feel pain at all; the infection can therefore go unnoticed until the skin has broken down and become visibly infected.

What causes diabetic foot?

Several risk factors contribute to the development of serious foot problems in diabetics.

Poorly fitted shoes are a common cause of foot problems in diabetics. If the patient develops blisters, corns, calluses, sore spots, or experiences pain that is associated with their footwear, they must obtain a new pair and undertake required treatment to prevent infections.

In the case of common foot abnormalities such as hammer toes, bunions, claw toe or flat feet, special shoe inserts may be necessary to prevent complications.

Peripheral neuropathy (PN) may also be the underlying cause of diabetic foot. Normally associated with poorly controlled diabetes, PN in the feet may lead to the loss of feeling in the limb, which will make it difficult for the patient to take notice when their shoes rub hard against the foot, or a foot strain. This will lead to formation of corns and calluses on the foot which in diabetes patients may result in infections if not immediately treated. A diabetic patient may also fail to notice when a stone enters their shoes. Due to the loss of sensitivity in the foot nerves, the stone may continuously rub against the foot when walking, creating a sore on the foot.

Poor blood circulation, particularly in severe cases and inappropriately controlled diabetes will lead to the narrowing and hardening of blood vessels in the feet making it difficult for white blood cells to fight infections.

Trauma to the foot, in any form, may increase the risk of developing a foot problem in diabetics.

Fungal infections of the skin and toenails are common causes for serious bacterial infections if not treated right. Similarly, ingrown toenails may result in complications for diabetics if not treated by a specialist.

Smoking damages blood vessels and decreases the ability of the body to deliver oxygen. This will disrupt healing and constitutes a major risk factor for infections and amputation.

Diabetic foot symptoms

There are several symptoms that diabetics may experience when their condition affects the feet.

Persistent pain can be a symptom of a bruise, sprain, overuse, improperly fitting shoes or it may be a sign of an underlying infection. Infections may be accompanied by redness or swelling of the feet. Localised warmth may signal inflammation, perhaps from wounds that won't heal, or that heal very slowly. The patient may experience fever or chills in association with a wound on the foot, which may signal a life-threatening condition.

When neuropathy occurs as a result of damaged nerves, the patient may experience loss of feeling in the affected limb.

Pain in the legs and buttocks, particularly when walking, is a sign of peripheral vascular disease. When foot infections in diabetes start to develop, poor venous circulation may result from it; the patient will notice the skin becoming hard, shiny and hairless. Wounds will fail to heal as the white blood cells will not enter the infected area, due to blocked arteries. The skin may crack and peel due to the loss of nerves that control the moisture and oil content.

Calluses build up faster and more often for people who suffer from diabetes. If not treated by a specialist, the skin will thicken, crack and may cause further complications.

The poor circulation and the damaged nerves associated with diabetic feet are at the base of the high number of amputations that result from foot infections related to diabetes.

Treatment for diabetic foot

The medical treatment for diabetic foot problems depends on the underlying conditions that caused it.

If the doctor determines that a wound or ulcer on the patient's foot is infected, or is at risk of becoming infected, he or she will prescribe antibiotics to treat the infection. For limb-threatening infections, the patient may be admitted to hospital and administered intravenous antibiotics. Less serious conditions may be treated with medication as an outpatient.

The patient may be referred to the wound care centre if diabetic wounds and ulcers are particularly severe and require a special treatment plan. This can include surgical debridement of the wound, improvement of blood circulation through surgery or therapy, special dressings, antibiotics, or even a combination of treatments.

In the case of bone abnormalities, toenail and other foot problems such as corns, calluses, hammer toes, flat feet, heel spurs, bunions or arthritis, the patient may be referred to an orthopaedic surgeon. They will recommend special footwear, prescribe orthotics or shoe inserts, remove corns and calluses and, if necessary, surgically remove bunions and other underlying bone problems that can be life-threatening when combined with diabetes.

Your doctor will also make recommendations in terms of home health care, or recommend a home nurse to assist with changing dressings, monitor blood sugar and assist the patient with the administration of antibiotics and other prescribed medications.

Home care recommendations may include footwear solutions, lotions to keep the skin on the feet moist, toenail trimming and ways to reduce, or quit smoking.

Diabetic neuropathy

Diabetic neuropathy is a complication of diabetes that manifests itself through loss of sensation, most commonly in the feet, due to nerve injuries. Nerve injuries are a cause of the high levels of sugar in the blood combined with a decreased blood flow.

Diabetic neuropathy can be extremely painful and cause a huge deal of discomfort. In most cases it is accompanied by loss of sensation, or 'numbness' in the feet, which may also become permanent.

Diabetic neuropathy in the feet develops slowly and worsens in time. It usually takes months, even years for the condition to become severe. In other words, the older the patient gets and the longer they are diabetic, the more likely they are to develop neuropathy.

What causes diabetic neuropathy?

Diabetic neuropathy is caused by abnormal levels of blood sugar. Over time, high blood sugar levels tend to damage blood vessels and nerves, which is why people unable to control their blood sugar may later in life develop the condition. High glucose weakens the capillaries and threatens the supply of oxygen and nutrients to the nerves. Nerves are therefore unable to transmit signals.

Alcoholism is a common cause for diabetic neuropathy; cigarette smoking and high cholesterol are also major risk factors.

Inflammation in the nerves also causes diabetic neuropathy. It occurs when the immune system mistakenly attacks a part of the body, treating it like a foreign organism.

Genetic factors that are not related to diabetes may make an individual susceptible to developing diabetic neuropathy.

Age is another factor in diabetic neuropathy development. People who've suffered from diabetes for more than 25 years are more susceptible to nerve damage.

Height may also influence the development of diabetic neuropathy. Tall people are more prone to it because they have longer peripheral nerves.

Nerve injury may also cause diabetic neuropathy. Whether they get damaged through inflammation or mechanical injuries, nerves become vulnerable to neuropathy and lose the ability to transmit signals to the brain.

Symptoms of diabetic neuropathy

Symptoms of diabetic neuropathy usually develop slowly over years. They normally start in the toes and slowly move up the legs. Diabetic neuropathy affects both legs equally.

The immediate symptom of diabetic neuropathy is the loss of sensation in the feet, making the patient irresponsive to pain or temperature changes. Injuries to the foot will not hurt as much as expected and will not heal, or heal really slowly. Tingling and burning sensations may occur.

Nerve injuries are often accompanied by muscle atrophy (reduction in muscle size), which will make walking difficult, often painful. At night there might be jabbing sensations of pain occurring. Rarely, severe cases of painful neuropathy may lead to hypersensitivity in the feet when even the touch of a sheet can cause agonising pain.

Infections, foot ulcers, bone deformities, joint pain and other forms of foot problems are also symptoms of diabetic neuropathy.

Treatments for diabetic neuropathy

There is no known treatment to reverse neuropathy. Patients with diabetes must control their disease through medical supervision and be aware of the risk factors related to diabetic neuropathy.

Depending on the symptoms, several treatment options may be considered to slow progression by keeping the blood sugar levels under control. Taking insulin as prescribed, maintaining a diet for diabetes, exercising, and visiting a doctor regularly represent initial treatment steps for all diabetics.

When the condition causes muscle atrophy, this may be tacked by the use of braces for support. Physical therapy enables the maintenance of muscle strength.

Medications are administered when the high level of glucose induces pain. Painful diabetic neuropathy is chronic and sometimes progresses to debilitating levels. Antidepressants and antiepileptics are used to relieve pain. Codeine is sometimes prescribed as a short-term solution for pain relief. Capsaicin (a topical cream) is now available for the same purpose. However, no patient ever experiences complete pain relief. Where the treatment achieves a 50% pain reduction, it is deemed successful.

Although not yet confirmed as a treatment for diabetic neuropathy, acupuncture may also help relieve pain. Transcutaneous electrical nerve stimulation (TENS) is a type of therapy that applies pulses of electricity to the nerves to reduce the pain caused by diabetic neuropathy.

Appropriate foot care is also recommended.

Other forms of treatment and neuropathic pain relief include hypnosis, relaxation training and applications of analgesic creams to relieve muscle and joint pain associated with diabetic neuropathy.

Foot ulcer

A foot ulcer is an open sore on the foot.

A foot ulcer can be a shallow red crater that involves only the surface skin. A foot ulcer also can be very deep. A deep foot ulcer may be a crater that extends through the full thickness of the skin. It may involve tendons, bones and other deep structures.

People with diabetes and people with poor circulation are more likely to develop foot ulcers. It can be difficult to heal a foot ulcer. In people with these conditions, even a small foot ulcer can become infected if it does not heal quickly.

If an infection occurs in an ulcer and is not treated right away, it can develop into:

- An abscess (a pocket of pus).

- A spreading infection of the skin and underlying fat (cellulitis).

- A bone infection (osteomyelitis).

- Gangrene (an area of dead, darkened body tissue caused by poor blood flow).

Among people with diabetes, most severe foot infections that ultimately require some part of the toe, foot or lower leg to be amputated start as a foot ulcer.

What causes a foot ulcer?

Foot ulcers are especially common in people who have one or more of the following health problems:

- Peripheral neuropathy. This is nerve damage in the feet or lower legs. Diabetes is the most common cause of peripheral neuropathy. When nerves in the feet are damaged, they can no longer warn about pain or discomfort. When this happens, tight-fitting shoes can trigger a foot ulcer by rubbing on a part of the foot that has become numb. People with peripheral neuropathy may not be able to feel when they've stepped on something sharp or when they have an irritating pebble in their shoes, for example. They can injure their feet significantly and never know it, unless they examine their feet routinely for injury.

- Vision problems, as elderly people and diabetics can't see their feet well enough to examine them for problems.

- Circulatory problems. Any illness that decreases circulation to the feet can cause foot ulcers. Less blood reaches the feet, which deprives cells of oxygen. This makes the skin more vulnerable to injury. And it slows the foot's ability to heal.

- Peripheral artery disease (poor circulation in the leg arteries). It also causes pain in the leg or buttock during walking.

- Abnormalities in the bones or muscles of the feet. Any condition that distorts the normal anatomy of the foot can lead to foot ulcers. This is particularly true if the foot is forced into shoes that don't fit the foot's altered shape. Examples are claw feet, feet with fractures, and cases of severe arthritis.

More than any other group, people with diabetes have a particularly high risk of developing foot ulcers. This is because the long-term complications of diabetes often include neuropathy and circulatory problems. Without prompt and proper treatment, a foot ulcer may require hospital treatment. Or, it may lead to deep infection, or gangrene and amputation.

In addition to diabetes, other medical conditions can increase the risk of foot ulcers.

Symptoms of a foot ulcer

A foot ulcer looks like a red crater in the skin. Most foot ulcers are located on the side or bottom of the foot or on the top or tip of a toe. This round crater can be surrounded by a border of thickened, callused skin. This border may develop over time. In very severe ulcers, the red crater may be deep enough to expose tendons or bones.

If the nerves in the foot are functioning normally, then the ulcer will be painful. If not, then a person with a foot ulcer may not know it is there, particularly if the ulcer is located on a less obvious portion of the foot.

In disabled or elderly patients, a relative or caregiver may be the one who becomes aware of the problem. The caregiver may notice that foot looks red and swollen. There may be drainage on the sock and a foul odour.

In most cases, your doctor can tell that you have a foot ulcer simply by looking at your foot.

If you have diabetes, your doctor will assess your control of your blood sugar. He or she will ask about the care that you take to keep your feet healthy. The doctor will ask about the type of shoes that you usually wear.

Your doctor will evaluate the ulcer to determine:

- How deep the ulcer is.
- Whether there is an infection.
- Whether you have any foot abnormalities, circulatory problems or neuropathy that will interfere with healing.

Your doctor may ask you to walk as part of your examination. This is because your walking pattern (gait) may highlight knee and ankle abnormalities that cause abnormal pressure spots on the feet. Your doctor also will look for other foot problems, such as claw foot or fallen arches.

To check for neuropathy, your doctor may:

* Test the sensation in your feet.

* Check your reflexes.

* Use a tuning fork to see if you can feel the vibration in your toes.

Your doctor also can test the circulation in your legs and feet. He or she can do this by feeling your pulses and noting whether your feet are pink and warm. If your pulses are weakened, then your doctor may use Doppler ultrasound to test your circulation.

Your doctor may use a cotton swab or other thin probe to examine the ulcer itself. These tools can be used to see how deep the ulcer is, and they can help check for exposed tendons or bones. Your doctor will look closely for redness around the ulcer. A large margin of redness can be a sign of cellulitis.

Your doctor may order other tests to better understand the extent of the ulcer and to determine whether it is infected. These tests may include:

* Blood tests.

* Bacterial cultures of the ulcer.

* X-rays.

* Magnetic resonance imaging (MRI).

* A computed tomography (CT) scan.

* A bone scan.

Treatments for a foot ulcer

If you have good circulation in your foot, your doctor may treat your foot ulcer with a procedure called debridement. This consists of trimming away diseased tissue. He or she also will remove any nearby callused skin.

The doctor then will apply a dressing. He or she may prescribe specialised footwear to relieve pressure on the ulcerated area. This specialised footwear may be a cast. Or it may be a loosely fitting post-operative walking shoe or sandal that can be worn over a bandage.

Your doctor will need to see you frequently to examine and debride the area. A nurse may need to visit you to change the dressing every few days. Care of a foot ulcer can require multiple visits over weeks or months. The visits will last for as long as it takes for your ulcer to heal completely. If there is a possibility of infection, you may be given antibiotics.

Once the ulcer has healed, your doctor may prescribe roomy, well-cushioned footwear. This footwear should not put pressure on vulnerable areas of your feet. This will help to prevent ulcers in the future.

Foot ulcers that do not respond to more conservative therapy may require surgery. In certain situations, without leg surgery, the ulcer may not heal properly.

People with poor circulation may need vascular surgery. This is surgery to correct blood flow problems in the leg arteries. Usually, blood flow is re-routed through the leg using a bypass artery.

FAQs

Following are some frequently asked questions related to foot care and foot problems, answered by The Institute of Chiropodists and Podiatrists

What is the difference between a chiropodist and podiatrist?

There is no difference between a chiropodist and podiatrist. The 'old' title was chiropodist. It is thought the title 'podiatrist' more accurately reflects the professional role of the discipline.

I have heard that skin cancers are becoming more frequent on the foot and leg, is this true?

All types of skin cancer are increasing in the UK. The most dangerous type of skin cancer is malignant melanoma (a cancerous 'mole') because it can spread to parts of the body other than the skin. Most other skin cancers rarely spread beyond the patch of skin they are affecting, although they can in rare cases and so do need treating. The number of people aged 65 and over dying from malignant melanoma has almost tripled in the last 30 years in the UK (source: Cancer Research UK 2012).

In women, over 40% of malignant melanomas are on the leg and foot, so if you have a mole that is changing rapidly, develops an irregular outline, is getting bigger or changing colour then seek advice from a suitably qualified health professional. Remember, although most dark patches under a nail are bruises, a skin cancer can form under a toe or fingernail. In men the most common site is on the trunk. Bear in mind that not all health professionals have appropriate experience in skin cancers, including GPs, so if in doubt seek further confirmation by referral to a specialist.

The latest statistics (2012) from cancer research UK suggest a possible occurrence of just over 11 cases of malignant melanoma per 100,000 of the population and it is the commonest type of cancer in people aged 15 to 34. Rapid treatment is the key to a happy outcome, so if you have concerns, get the mole checked.

An excellent source of information is the website of Skcin, the UK's leading skin cancer charity: www.skcin.org

Will I qualify for free treatment and do I have to see a doctor to be referred?

You do not need a referral to a chiropodist/podiatrist, but your doctor may wish to refer you. Free treatments are available in some areas but this is *not* the general rule. Your practitioner will advise you.

How do I know that the chiropodist has the relevant training?

All podiatrists/chiropodists must be registered with the HPC as it is a criminal offence for non-registered persons to use these protected titles. You can validate your practitioner's qualification at www.hpc-uk.org

How much can I expect to pay for basic treatment?

Professional fees vary from area to area, therefore it is best to check around. Do, however, be mindful that you need a professionally trained practitioner working with you.

People call a doctor of podiatry for help diagnosing and treating a wide array of foot and ankle problems. Please contact a professional if you experience one of the following:

- Persistent pain in your feet or ankles.
- Changes in the nails or skin on your foot.
- Severe cracking, scaling or peeling on the heel or foot.
- Blisters on your feet.

There are signs of bacterial infection, including:

- Increased pain, swelling, redness, tenderness or heat.
- Red streaks extending from the affected area.
- Discharge or pus from an area on the foot.
- Foot or ankle symptoms that do not improve after two weeks of treatment with a non-prescription product.

- Spreading of an infection from one area of the foot to another, such as under the nail bed, skin under the nail, the nail itself, or the surrounding skin.

- Thickening toenails that cause discomfort.

- Heel pain accompanied by a fever, redness (sometimes warmth), or numbness.

- Tingling in the heel; persistent heel pain without putting any weight or pressure on your heel.

- Pain that is not alleviated by ice or over-the-counter painkillers (such as aspirin, ibuprofen or acetaminophen).

- Diabetics with poor circulation who develop athlete's foot.

Glossary

Achilles tendon
Long, strong tendon in the back of the leg, which attaches the calf muscle to the heel.

Adipose
Fat tissue.

Anterior tibialis
Muscle that begins in the lower leg and moves the foot upwards.

Athlete's foot
Fungal infection. Also called tinea pedis.

Bunion
Bony prominence on the inside edge of the great toe usually associated with a hallux valgus deformity (big toe is angled away from the midline).

Bursa
A sac containing a tiny amount of fluid present where friction needs to be minimised, such as a tendon or skin gliding over a bony prominence. Best thought of as a deflated balloon containing several drops of oil. The most obvious bursa sac is beneath the loose skin behind the elbow.

Bursitis
Inflammation of a bursal sac.

Callus
Thickening of the outer layer of skin due to irritation or pressure.

Cavus foot
High arches.

Cellulitis
Inflammation of the skin often associated with a localised infection of the skin.

Claw toe
Curling of the lesser toes whereby both small joints of a toe are flexed.

Corn
A thickening of the normal keratin of the skin. Corns are either hard (helomata dura) and usually on top of the toes, or soft (helomata mollia) and between the toes.

Crepitus
Grinding most often produced by joint surfaces not being smooth.

Degenerative
Having the tendency to deteriorate, or implying a wear and tear process.

Dermis
The deeper layer of the skin containing nerves, blood vessels and sweat glands.

Diabetes
A complex disease, affecting multiple organ systems, due to insulin deficiency resulting in a high blood glucose level.

Distal
Farthest away from the trunk or center of the body. Opposite of the term 'proximal'.

Dysplasia
From the Greek 'dys' meaning 'bad' and 'plasis' meaning 'a molding'. It is a very general term used to mean any abnormal tissue development.

Epidermis
Outer layer of the skin.

Fascia
Tough fibrous tissue enveloping muscles and separating them into various compartments.

Fibula
The smaller and more lateral of the two long bones of the lower leg.

Gait
Manner of walking. Can be normal or abnormal, such as antalgic (painful) gait where the stance phase is shortened.

Ganglion
A non-cancerous cyst filled with a clear gelatinous-like material.

Gout
Arthritic condition caused by excessive uric acid in the bloodstream.

Great toe
The largest toe of the foot. Also called the hallux.

Hagland's deformity
Bony prominence of the heel, near where the Achilles tendon attaches to the heel bone.

Hallux
The great or largest toe.

Hallux valgus
A lateral deviation of the great toe, based at the metatarsal phalangeal joint.

Hammer toe
Curling of the lesser toes, characterised by flexion of the first joint (PIP joint) and extension of the metatarsal phalangeal (MTP) joint. Very similar to a claw toe deformity.

Heel spurs
Growths of bone on the underside of the foot in the area of the heel bone.

Haematoma
A collection of blood outside of a blood vessel.

Idiopathic
Isolated abnormality without obvious causes.

Ingrown nail
Abnormality of the nail penetrating the skin just past the nail grooves.

Instep
Arched middle portion of the human foot, especially the upper (dorsal) aspect.

Inter-phalangeal joints
Joints between the bones of the toe.

Lateral
On the side (outside) or furthest away from the midline of the body, (opposite is 'medial').

Ligament
Attaches bone to bone, thus stabilising joints.

Mallet toe
Flexed deformity of the last joint of a toe, accompanied by a callus at the tip of that toe.

Metatarsalgia
Pain under the metatarsal heads in the forefoot usually directly or indirectly resulting from repetitive localised overload of this area of the foot.

Metatarsal adductus
Congenital curving inward of the feet.

Metatarsals
Long bones of the midfoot proximal to the toes (phalanges). They are numbered from one to five, five being behind the little toe.

Magnetic resonance imaging (MRI)
An advanced X-ray technique that can visualise not only bones, but soft tissue, ligaments, tendons and cartilage.

Muscle
Specialised tissue that, because of its contractility, moves joints by its attachment to bone via the tendon.

Neuroma
Generally implies a thickened and irritated nerve, as seen between the toes in a Morton's neuroma.

Non-invasive treatment
A procedure which does not involve entering the body.

NSAIDs (non-steroidal anti-inflammatory drugs)
NSAIDs are a class of medication that often serve to decrease pain symptoms by dampening the body's inflammatory response.

Oedema
Swelling.

Orthopaedics
The medical specialty devoted to the diagnosis, treatment, rehabilitation and prevention of injuries of your musculoskeletal system.

Orthosis
Device which a person wears or uses to help support, align or accommodate a body part.

Osteoarthritis
Arthritis characterised by partial or complete loss of the cartilage (articular cartilage) covering a joint.

Peripheral nerves
Nerves in the arms or legs, as opposed to those in or near the spinal cord and brain.

Pes planus
Flat feet. It is commonly found in patients who develop symptomatic acquired adult flat foot deformity.

Phalanges
Small bones that make up the toes,

Plantar
The sole of the foot.

Plantar fascia
Strong fibrous tissue attached to the heel, extended along the sole and attached at the metatarsal heads.

Plantar wart
A verucca.

Podiatrist
A podiatric physician, Doctor of Podiatric Medicine (DPM), specialising in treatment and conditions of the foot and ankle.

Pronation
Turning out of the hindfoot. It is often associated with a flat foot.

Prosthesis
Device which replaces or substitutes for a body part.

Rheumatoid arthritis
Swelling, discomfort and stiffness of the joints and tendons, often beginning in the feet. This may be accompanied by the formation of rheumatoid nodules in the soft tissues.

Sesamoids
A bone which is enveloped within a tendon, as in the two bones under the first metatarsal bone.

Shin splints
Leg pain around the shin bone (tibia) occurring after a period of activity.

Sprain
An injury to the ligaments holding a joint together. For example, an ankle sprain is an injury to the ligament(s) stabilising the outside of the ankle joint.

Supination
An inward turning of the foot. The opposite of pronation.

Talus
The talus is the main bone that helps connect the lower leg to the foot.

Talipes equinovarus
Also called 'clubfoot'. It is a congenital condition where the soles of a newborn face each other.

Tarsals
The bones that make up the heel and the back of the instep. There are seven tarsals in each foot. Together with the metatarsals, they form the arch of the foot.

Tarsal tunnel syndrome
A condition characterised by irritation of the tibial nerve behind the medial malleolus (inside of the ankle).

Tendon
Band of strong fibres which connect muscle to bone.

Tendonitis
Inflammation of the tendon tissue or the sheath around a tendon.

Trauma
Either direct or indirect. Indirect trauma results when the force is applied away from the actual part injured, such as a twisting motion. Direct trauma results when the force is fully directed at the injured part, such as being struck by a bat.

Help List

Andrew Stanley
The Rebound Clinic
www.reboundclinic.co.uk
Podiatrist and running biomechanics specialist.

The British Foot and Ankle Society
www.bofas.org.uk

The British Footwear Association
www.britishfootwearassociation.co.uk

Family Doctor
www.family-doctor.org.uk
Register of family doctors.

Feet First
www.feetfirstworldwide.com
A aharity to treat and prevent physical disability worldwide.

Hamish Dow (foot care specialist)
The Dow Clinic
www.thedowclinic.co.uk

Institute of Chiropodists and Podiatrists
www.iocp.org.uk

Life's 2 Good
www.lifes2good.co.uk
Specialist foot care products.

Neo-G

www.neo-g.co.uk
Specialist foot care products.

NHS Direct

www.nhsdirect.nhs.uk
The UK health advice and information service.

Skcin

www.skcin.org
The UK's leading skin cancer charity.

Scholl

www.scholl.com
Specialist foot care products.

The Society for Chiropodists and Podiatrists

www.feetforlife.org

Steps

www.steps-charity.org.uk
A charity supporting children and adults affected by a lower limb condition such as clubfoot or a hip condition.

UK Group of Specialist Hospitals

www.uk-sh.co.uk